"As you live the Christian life,
you may have periods
of darkness or of doubt.
You may encounter painful struggle
and discouragement.
But there will also be moments
of exultation and glory. And most important of all,
you will become free."

Books by John White

The Cost of Commitment
Daring to Draw Near
Eros Defiled
Excellence in Leadership
The Fight
Flirting with the World
The Golden Cow
Healing the Wounded (with Ken Blue)
The Masks of Melancholy
Parables (LifeGuide Bible Study)
Parents in Pain
Putting the Soul Back in Psychology
The Race
When the Spirit Comes with Power

The Archives of Anthropos by John White

The Tower of Geburah
The Iron Sceptre
The Sword Bearer

Booklets by John White

Bible Study
Prayer

JohnWhite

THE FIGHT

A PRACTICAL HANDBOOK FOR CHRISTIAN LIVING

INTERVARSITY PRESS
DOWNERS GROVE, ILLINOIS 60515

To Alec Clifford
without whose encouragement
I would never have
written for publication

InterVarsity Press
P.O. Box 1400, Downers Grove, IL 60515
World Wide Web: www.ivpress.com
E-mail: mail@ivpress.com

InterVarsity Press® *is the book-publishing division of InterVarsity Christian Fellowship/USA*®, *a student
movement active on campus at hundreds of universities, colleges and schools of nursing in the United States of
America, and a member movement of the International Fellowship of Evangelical Students. For information
about local and regional activities, write Public Relations Dept., InterVarsity Christian Fellowship/USA, 6400
Schroeder Rd., P.O. Box 7895, Madison, WI 53707-7895.*

Cover illustration: Jerry Tiritilli
ISBN 0-87784-777-0

Printed in the United States of America ∞

43	42	41	40	39	38	37	36	35	34	33	32	31	30
14	13	12	11	10	09	08	07	06	05	04	03	02	

Contents

1/Beginnings   11
A New Status before God   12
New Relationships with God and People   14
A Foe of Legions   16
A Passage to Study   17

2/Prayer   19
Deep Calls to Deep   20
God in Search of Man   23
Prayer Language   27
Praying in Public   31
Hearing God's Voice   32
The Bible and Prayer   33
Daydreaming   34
The Practice of the Presence   35
Summary   36
A Few Suggestions   36

3/God Still Speaks   39
Practical Problems   43
How to Study   46

Translations and Paraphrases   48
The Time Factor   51
Setting a Goal   55
A Few Suggestions   56

4/On Being a Signpost   59
The Nature of Signposts   61
Salesman for Christ?   64
On Being Real   67
How Real Was Peter?   69
Hostile Reactions   72
The Need to Know More   74
Summary   75
A Passage to Study   76

5/His Infernal Majesty   77
Temptation without Dismay   78
Accusation of the Brethren   82
Deception Overcome   89
Warfare with the Devourer   91
A Passage to Study   96

6/Faith   97
Man's Response to God's Initiative   97
The Invisible and Hoped For   100
Increasing Your Faith   102
Recalling Bad Times   105
Remembering the Promises   107
Getting Rid of Excess Baggage   110
Being Tried by Fire   111
A Passage to Study   118

7/Changed Relationships   121
The Biological Family   121
The Family: A Script to Follow, a Score to Dance   124
The Family of God   129
Finding a Church Home   132
Too Many Meetings   135

The We/They Dichotomy   137
The Heart of Christian Fellowship   140
Making It Work   142
That We All May Be One   148

8/Guidance   153
The General Nature of Guidance   154
Scripture and Guidance   157
The Persuasive Power of Desire   158
Guidance and Gifts   161
Counsel, Circumstances and Fleeces   164
The Voice of the Shepherd   169
Prerequisites for Guidance   172
Passages to Study   176

9/Holiness   179
The God Who Is Holy   180
Peace and Holiness   182
Crisis or Growth?   188
God's Work or Yours?   190
The Holy Spirit   194
A Passage to Study   199

10/Deliverance from Drudgery   201
Craftsmanship, Technology and Cramming for Exams   202
Easy and Light   207
The Secular and the Profane   209
Witness through Success?   210
Organizing Your Time   212
Loaves and Fishes   213
A Passage to Study   214

11/The Fight   215
The Battle with the World   218
The Battle against the Flesh   221
The Battle against the Powers of Darkness   222
The Spirit and the Battle   224
The Last Enemy   226

1

Beginnings

When you became a Christian, a number of extremely important events took place both in heaven and in your own body.

You may or may not have felt anything. Christians have widely differing experiences, ranging from intense emotions to nothing at all. You may not even be able to say when you became a Christian. All you may know is that at this moment you acknowledge the Jesus of history to be your Savior and your God.

Yet whatever you felt or did not feel and whether or not you know when you became a Christian, the events I speak of took place. As I describe them I shall, in a way, be defining what a Christian is.

Purely psychological events occur in all varieties of conversion. Had you been converted to communism or to any religion or world view, you would have experienced them. The psychological factors have been long recognized and well described. They consist of temporary "feeling states" and a turn around in a person's understanding of life.

In Christian conversion, as in any other conversion, you

may experience many such psychological events and you will certainly experience a change in life view. What makes Christian conversion different is that supernatural events also occur. The feeling states in non-Christian conversion are temporary. They are equally temporary in Christian conversion.

But the supernatural, and often unfelt, events are permanent. They mark you in the sight of demons and angels as a human who is different. They bring your body into touch with eternity and with the Eternal God.

A New Status before God

In the first place, you have been *justified.* This is to say that God looks upon you and deals with you *as though you were perfectly righteous,* as though you had never sinned and will never sin. However difficult this idea may be for you to grasp, it represents an event that has already taken place and that will never change.

It is not that God wears blinders and pretends you are better than you are. He knows about your sin. Yet his feelings toward you and his dealings with you are based on a righteousness Christ has given you. God treats you as though you were as righteous as Jesus. You may be uncomfortable with this idea. I shall deal with it more fully later on. As the impact of it breaks over your understanding you will marvel. Far from wanting to sin you will sense how you have been set free to be holy.

Your justification is both a heavenly event and a time-space event. It is a heavenly event insofar as Jesus is at this moment on the right hand of God's throne acting as your personal guarantor and representative. It is a heavenly event, too, in that your name is now recorded in the "not guilty" annals of heaven. It is an earthly event since you, a creature of time and space, may boldly step into the presence of the God of eternity and hold a conversation with him. Indeed you are encouraged to do so. Notice, you are not given permission to *crawl* into God's presence but to approach him with your head held high.

A second event that took place in your body is what is known as *regeneration* or new birth. By this event, eternity invaded space and re-established permanent links between your personality and the Eternal. Again, you may have experienced little or nothing when this most profound event occurred. By a miracle of divine grace a nonbiological life was implanted in you. It is a form of life that will enable you one day to inhabit eternity just as your biological life now enables you to live in time-space.

The life that entered you was the life of God himself. Your earthly parents gave life from their living bodies which became your life when you were born. In the same way God, in imparting to you his own life, became in very deed your heavenly Father. You are a child of God in a *literal*, not a metaphorical sense.

But the life must grow and develop. As it does so you will reflect, more and more, the likeness of the Father from whom the life came, just as some degree of likeness to your physical parents accompanies growth in your physical and emotional life. As God's life within you grows, it will influence both your emotional and your physical development. You will become more mature emotionally. Other things being equal, you will enjoy better physical health. Your new birth does not guarantee that you will never be emotionally or physically sick, but it will move you in the direction of improved health.

For your new life to grow, it must be fed and exercised. The food it requires is the Holy Scriptures. Exercise will consist of obedience by faith to the commands of God. You will also need to breathe deep drafts of heavenly air as your prayer life develops. All of these factors which contribute to your spiritual growth will be examined carefully in the chapters that follow. For the present it is enough to know that you are a hybrid—a being with two types of life and two sets of parentage.

New Relationships with God and People

As we have already begun to see, the events that have occurred to you include dramatic changes in your personal relationships. Once alienated from God, you have changed to being at peace with him as well as being his child. Christ, his unique Son whom you may formerly have ignored, now has a relationship with you, and you with him, which is many-faceted. He is your Shepherd and you are his sheep. As time goes on you will become increasingly expert at discerning his voice and being able to follow wherever he leads. On his part he guarantees you refreshment and rest, provided you follow him, and a determination to bring you back to the flock should you stray and get lost.

He is also your master, and you his slave. He always had the right to treat you as a slave, but he never whipped you into submission. Implicit in your new relationship is a recognition on your part that you *are* his slave and will allow him the right to govern your entire life. For though he demands obedience, he will still never force it. You have the power to deny him his rights. In doing so you would violate your commitment to him and damage your spiritual well-being. You would dishonor him. Nevertheless, he refuses either to turn you into an automaton or to be brutal to you.

He is also your priest, your "great high priest." When you come to the Father, you do so because of his offices. At those times when feelings of weakness and frustration crush you, you will find fresh courage when you remember your high priest is still human as well as divine. Having personally experienced every human temptation and stress, he can understand how you feel. He sympathizes with your weakness. Because of his eternal humanness, he is uniquely equipped both to support you and to plead for you.

We could discuss many facets of your relationship with Christ. He is your captain in battle and you his soldier. He is the bread on whom you feed. He is the light illuminating your interior darkness. And so we could go on. What in essence all of this means is that you now belong to him and he to you in a relationship of vital interchanges. Bonds have been established between you that nothing in heaven, earth or hell can break.

Many of your other relationships have changed too. For instance, you are now part of an innumerable company of redeemed human beings, both here and beyond death. You are a co-citizen with martyrs and apostles. Though my words may conjure up in your mind visions of swords, robes and sandals, your heavenly citizenship also has to do with mundane relationships in everyday life.

If you were brought up in a large family, you may have noticed that it was more difficult to get on with your brothers and sisters (or perhaps with one or two of them) than with friends outside the family. At times of crisis (such as when bullies picked on your bratty kid brother), you would all unite. But at other times tensions would exist.

Do not be surprised then to discover tensions within your heavenly family. Your brothers and sisters in Christ are not perfect. After the first happy glow, during which you may idealize them, you will be shocked to discover bitterness, bickering and overt hostility in the Christian "family."

You will also discover that some Christians are stupid, ornery, tactless; "stuffed shirts," prudes, hypocrites and so on. Some will be bigoted advocates of totally unacceptable political positions, and others will slurp their soup or have bad breath. We shall come to the complex question of how you relate to them later on. For the present it is enough that you remember that God loves them even though you find it hard to. You must also be charitable enough to admit that there may be unattractive features in your own personality. You don't wear robes and sandals yourself.

Finally, you must realize that the same new life that is in you is in them. Look well at their faults and see for yourself that the miracle of new life does not guarantee beauty of character. The life needs to grow and develop. That is why I am writing my book. I feel a great urge inside me to share with you as much as I can of what is important in practical Christian living.

A Foe of Legions

You have also established a new relationship with the powers of darkness. Whatever you were before you became a Christian—straight, horoscope reader, witch, warlock or Satanist—you are now the sworn foe of the legions of hell.

Have no delusions about their reality or their hostility. But do not fear them. The God inside you terrifies them. They cannot touch you, let alone hurt you. But they can still seduce and they will try. They will also oppose you as you obey Christ. If you play it cool and decide not to be a fanatic about Christianity, you will have no trouble from them. But if you are serious about Christ being your Lord and God, you can expect opposition.

"Resist the devil," writes James, "and he will flee from you" (Jas. 4:7). Life with Jesus can be an exhilarating and reassuring experience of constant triumph over evil forces. But the battle never ends. I write more about this later on.

Yet I would be foolish to suppose that I could, by writing a book or you by reading it, ensure your steady Christian growth. What both of us must realize is that you have been given a personal tutor. His coming to you is the most important event associated with your becoming a Christian. Whether you felt his coming or not, the Holy Spirit has taken up his dwelling place in you. Christ's object in sending him was to insure that you get even better instruction than the apostles had by having Jesus in their midst. You may lament the fact that Jesus is no longer here physically. But as Jesus sees it, you have a greater privilege by having God's Spirit inside you.

The Holy Spirit is a self-effacing person. He does not wish to tell you much about himself, preferring rather to instruct you about Christ and your relationship with him. You can learn about the Holy Spirit by reading certain passages in John's Gospel, which are listed at the end of this chapter. It is the Holy Spirit who will make truth come alive for you by enabling you to grasp it clearly, by reminding you of things he has previously taught you, by drilling you in difficult exercises that get at your personality weaknesses, by encouraging you when you are down, by echoing the good Shepherd's voice in your hearing and in many other ways.

If *he* uses my book, and far more important, the Scriptures, then you will make progress. If you rely on *him* rather than upon mechanical devices or religious exercises (both of which have a place) you will grow.

You may have periods of darkness or of doubt. You may encounter painful struggles and discouragement. But there will also be moments of exultation and glory. And most important of all, you will become free.

A Passage to Study
Don't read chapter two yet. Instead, spend half an hour quietly praying over the following passages. Make notes on them and try to answer the questions. Choose a modern translation if you have one.

Read John's Gospel (the fourth book in the New Testament), chapter 14, verses 15-26—these verses form part of Christ's final briefing session with the apostles.

1. Compare verse 16 (in which "another Counselor"

would come to the apostles and stay with them forever) with verse 18 and verse 20. We are told that the Holy Spirit, as well as being a person in his own right, is also the Spirit of Jesus and the Spirit of the Father. This is hard for us to grasp. What support would such an idea find in this passage?

2. What functions of the Holy Spirit are described here? Make a note of them and remember that the same Holy Spirit dwells in your body, too.

3. Read John chapter 15, verse 26 to chapter 16, verse 15. What further functions of the Holy Spirit are described? How would they apply in your own life?

4. In this chapter of my book I suggest that the Holy Spirit is self-effacing. What support does John's Gospel lend to this idea?

2

Prayer

When I was a medical student in England, someone in the Inter-Varsity group gave me a card which changed my life. The card was impressive. It was pale green, deepening to dark green at the edges. On it were a couple of quotations from the Gospels indicating how Jesus, on earth, once spent all night in prayer. Underneath the texts was one brief sentence ending, ". . . God helping me I resolve to spend at least twenty minutes daily in prayer to God." Below this was a dotted line where I signed my name.

The powerful appeal the card made to me must have had some explanation. It could have been its simplicity. The color and lettering certainly appealed to me aesthetically. Obviously there was more to it than either of these things, however. Thirty years have passed. Today a quiet song of joy is still flowing from my heart because of the on-going revolution that little green card began.

There are a number of ways of looking at it. I must have had a need in me, some inner longing to which the card appealed. Again, the need must have been met since my changed behavior has lasted long past my initial resolve.

Deep Calls to Deep

For the last ten years I have been watching the Manitoba spring. As snow melts, water trickles, then hurries into pools, lakes, floods. In front of our house a little lake stretches across the roadway to the delight of the small children and the annoyance of their seniors. There are drain openings on both sides of the street in the curbs of the sidewalks. The water is deepest by the drain openings. It affords me vast satisfaction every spring to plunge my hands into the cold water, seize the accumulation of dead leaves and twigs blocking the drain and then watch the eager rush of water into its thirsty jaws.

My little green card produced a release of that kind in my life. It unplugged me. I was set free.

I mention the fact because usually sermons on prayer stress either its importance or our Christian duty to pray. Indeed the implication of the words on my card was that if Jesus prayed, I ought to do so too. If he, the God-man, needed close contact with the Father in prayer, how much more did I?

Well it *is* our duty to pray and it *is* an important duty. The Scriptures themselves emphasize this. "Pray constantly" (1 Thess. 5:17). "In everything by prayer and supplication with thanksgiving let your requests be made known to God" (Phil. 4:6). "Pray at all times in the Spirit, with all prayer and supplication. To that end keep alert with all perseverance" (Eph. 6:18). "Men ought always to pray and not to faint" (Lk. 18:1).

But if all we knew was that it was our *duty* to pray or how important it was to pray, we would be in sorry straits. You can be earnest and duty-bound only so long—and after that the effort becomes intolerable. My card did not only stir my conscience into action. It awoke hope in me. I felt no pride as I signed it, only joy and a sense of expectation.

Years earlier I had attempted to pray. Dissatisfied with the quality of my Christian life and having read some (now forgotten) exhortation on prayer, I set my alarm for 6:00 A.M., determined to begin the day with two hours of prayer and Bible study. It was winter. English houses are not only dark but miserably cold in the early morning. My eyes were sore. My nose ran. I shivered and still felt dirty, even though I had washed and shaved. The silent house seemed strangely unfriendly. Determinedly I prayed—for my immediate family; for distant cousins, uncles, aunts; for neighbors and friends. Then I looked at my watch to find that only five minutes had gone by. Somehow I had to carry on for another hour and fifty-five minutes. Time stretched ahead like a cold eternity.

I managed to keep on praying for twenty-five minutes by which time I had exhausted every possible topic of prayer. A little uncertain of myself I decided that it might be appropriate to study the Bible. Not knowing where to start I elected to master Paul's Epistle to the Romans. I read with a vague sense of dissatisfaction. How did one *study* the Bible? I frowned and tried to concentrate, but the words stared back at me inscrutably, coldly determined to hold their own counsel.

Somehow I managed to go on frowning and reading for the rest of the two hours. But I was licked, and I knew it. I kept going for another two days, but on the third day I acknowledged my defeat and crawled miserably back to bed thirty-five minutes after I got up.

After that I put prayer and Bible study out of my mind. It was for saints and martyrs. I was not made of praying stuff. But I felt guilty, depressed and cheated.

For somewhere within me I had been hoping, even longing, for I knew not what. I had thought that by going through my performance of believing, sacrificial prayer, my longing would be satisfied. If satisfaction did not come to me, then my faith (or my capacity for sacrifice) was inadequate. The riches I craved were there. I yearned for them. But I was capable only of so much. So I stifled my longings.

But where had those longings come from? Did they represent an accumulation of frustrations for which I sought a magical and unrealistic answer? Was I being flung back to face "reality" and told to solve my problems in ways other than prayer-fantasies? Or was the longing divinely planted?

In the first chapter of Augustine's book *Confessions* are his oft-quoted words "for Thou hast made us for Thyself; and our hearts are restless, till they find their rest in Thee." Augustine's answer is the correct one. Frustrations we may have, but they are beside the point. We were designed for fellowship with God, and without that fellowship we ache in emptiness. He himself planted the longing there, a longing all of us share.

It may not always dominate your consciousness, but it is there. More than this, God plays his sweet music causing the longing to throb and come to life.

Deep within your vast interior spaces (and inner space and outer space are all one in eternity) is a tabernacle God built to commune with you. From it he calls you with tender urgency. And from the furthest reaches of your inner space an ache of yearning echoes back his call.

You may ignore it. At times you do so because the excitement of other attractions appeals to you more. But they appeal to the surface of your being. They create anxiety whereas his call is a call to peace.

Or perhaps you fear that you are unworthy to approach the tabernacle, much less to enter it. There seem so many apologies that you ought to make to God, so many problems, so much insincerity to overcome before you could begin to get close. And so you are alienated, living not only far from the God within you but far from the depths of your own being. You live on the surface of your life while Deep is calling to deep.

God in Search of Man

The first thing you must learn about prayer is that God wants fellowship with you and that he is drawing you to himself. To change the metaphor: He is pursuing you. He is waiting to trap you into an encounter with himself. He does so not because he needs you but because you need him. His is the tenderness of a mother over a fretful infant. Prayer is to turn inwardly (or outwardly—it is all one), enter the tabernacle where he waits and let him speak with you. For he is there. And he is speaking. And you may sit in quietness to drink in his beauty, trembling with joy.

But it may take time to learn the confidence of going into the presence of the One who calls you. Many books on prayer stress techniques for doing so. I believe only two things are necessary. First, you must recognize the Holy Spirit has already become your teacher. Don't ask *how* you can best cooperate with him. The teaching and training is *his* job, and in his own way and time he will teach you.

Second, you must let the truth of what I am saying sink into your heart in quietness. Remind yourself constantly of the words of Scripture: "Draw near to God and he will draw near to you" (Jas. 4:8). Memorize such verses of the Bible as:

Therefore, brethren, since we have confidence to enter the sanctuary by the blood of Jesus, by the new and living way which he opened for us ... and since we have a great priest over the house of God, let us draw near with a true heart in full assurance of faith, with our hearts sprinkled clean from an evil conscience. (Heb. 10:19-22)

Up to now in a roundabout sort of way, I have been trying to get two things across to you. First, the initiative in prayer lies with God. Second, you were designed to respond to his initiative. Your business and your deepest satisfaction will be to respond to the overtures that he, in his astonishing condescension, is making.

But I would expose you to two dangers were I to leave the matter there. First, I might leave you with the impression that all you need to do is to wait silently, by faith, and try to listen to God's voice. This is the lesser of the dangers and I will discuss it later. The other danger is that you might confuse prayer with something like Transcendental Meditation. For certainly what I have written opens the door to possibilities of unearthly rapture.

There is a fundamental difference between meditative techniques (involving exercises in breathing or in concentration upon one's physical body or in becoming preoccupied with a single object until it communicates itself to the whole field of one's consciousness). The object of such techniques is to achieve an altered state of consciousness—a relaxed, detached mental state sought for the well-being that may result from the exercise.

When a Christian prays, he is not aiming at an altered feeling state or state of consciousness. Nor when God calls us to pray does he offer us a trip. His aim is that we may have fellowship with him, a person who really exists. Whether altered states of consciousness or feelings accompany prayer is neither here nor there. Usually they don't except in some minor degree. Occasionally, like Paul, one may be "caught up ... into Paradise ... and (hear) things that cannot be told, which man may not utter" (2 Cor. 12:2-4).

Ecstasy may come rarely and to a few, but it is never to be sought. It is no mark of special favor. What must be sought is fellowship with a real person. And this brings me to the first problem I raised.

As I wait in silence I am not opening my being to a Mysterious Unknown. I am listening for the God of the Scriptures, the God whose tabernacle has been built in my innermost being. And as I penetrate that sanctuary I will encounter the God whom Jesus revealed and whom the Scriptures describe. It is to the One who has revealed himself already that I must come.

An unknown English mystic of the twelfth century wrote a profoundly influential book known as *The Cloud* or *Cloud of the Unknowing*. It is still available in paperback. I meditated long and prayerfully on *Cloud*, and as I did so I saw clearly where true Christianity and some forms of mysticism part company. The author of *Cloud* exhorts us to put all that we know about God under the dark Cloud of Unknowing, stripping ourselves of every idea or concept of God, confessing that we cannot know, except as we penetrate into the blackness with "the pure intent of naked love."

Sounds great. It has "blown the minds" of people of profound devotion and brilliant intellect for the past eight hundred years. And it is true that we cannot understand the God we approach in prayer. His thoughts are not our thoughts. His ways surpass our capacity to grasp. Because he transcends all we can understand or know, we speak of the *transcendence* of God. But we are not invited to know what cannot be known until a coming day. And if God has gone to such pains, through the prophets and by means of the incarnation, to reveal to us what we can understand of him, is it not irreverent folly and vanity to cast aside all that he has revealed at such cost for the vain benefit of a supposed "higher" experience? All we may be achieving is the same altered states of consciousness that I have been talking about.

The God of the universe has made himself comprehensible to our finite minds. The God of the Scriptures seeks fellowship with us. He will always remain mysterious, but it will be the mystery of our dearly loved, truly known Father. (What child *understands* the earthly father he knows so intimately?)

Therefore, be simple and practical in your approach to God. Have a look at your daily schedule and see where and how you can arrange for twenty minutes of unhurried, quiet waiting on God every day. Choose a place where you are unlikely to be distracted and go there regularly.

There is nothing magical about a time span of twenty minutes. It is a starting point that most inexperienced pray-ers find helpful. You need about that length of time so as to be unrushed, unhurried. If you later find you need more time, no problem.

Begin by remembering that he seeks you and longs to speak with you. If you feel fuddle-headed first thing in the morning, wash and dress before your "quiet time." Should you still feel flat as lukewarm coke, don't worry. Simply begin by thanking God that whether you feel him or not, you know he has been waiting for you. Then instruct your soul repeatedly as the psalmist did: "For God alone my soul waits in silence, for my hope is from him" (Ps. 62:5).

How you proceed from there will depend on what you discover, under the Spirit's gentle guidance, to be helpful.

The Spirit will teach you *worship* which means expressing to God how worthy he is. He will also teach you *praise* and *thanksgiving*. Some of the psalms may be helpful here. There is nothing wrong with reading one of them aloud as an act of worship to God. Some of them (such as Ps. 30:1-3) may express your feelings better than your own words can.

You may even find that some of the great prayers of the past (like those of Lancelot Andrewes) are helpful. Or you may be freer expressing praise and worship in your own words.

Confession of sin is not only helpful but essential if your relationship to God is to remain clear. But I would like to deal with the whole matter of confession and a cleansed conscience in a later chapter, developing some of the ideas we began to look at in chapter one.

Talking over problems, *supplications* (asking for things you want), *intercessions* (asking things for other people) are all part of prayer. The thing to remember is that God is intensely interested in the smallest details of your own and other people's lives. To realize this does not make one's prayers self-centered, but paradoxically it is a way to avoid the danger of self-centeredness.

Are there things about God or the Bible that trouble you? Are you upset over the injustices and hypocrisies of those around you? God cares. He wants you to share these things with him. As you do so you will begin to marvel at an infinite God who is concerned with your petty problems and who does not dismiss them as petty. Because they are important to you, they are to him too.

As for your personal requests, he has already anticipated them. He is waiting for you to make them. You do not have to twist his arm. I personally wait eagerly for my children to come to me to ask me for their allowances or to request me to read a story. When they fail to ask, I am disappointed. God has, unknown to you, been encouraging you to make some requests before you ever began to formulate them in your mind. And as for other requests which it would be wrong of him to grant you, he is only too happy that you have the confidence to be frank about them.

For prayer is not *you* trying to move *God*. Prayer is among other things *being caught up* into God's directions and activity. He orders the affairs of the universe, and he invites you to participate by prayer. Intercession is God and you in partnership, bringing his perfect plans into being.

Prayer Language
What words ought you to use in prayer? Do you say "Thee"

and "Thou" or "You" when addressing God? Ought one always to end prayer with the words, "In the name of the Lord Jesus Christ. Amen"?

There are no rules. God is not concerned with the form of your words but with the honesty and reverence of your heart. The more he teaches you about himself and the more aware you become of him, the more your words and attitude will be appropriate. Let God make you aware of himself, then be yourself in the presence of the Holy One.

As for using the words, "in the name of Jesus," everything depends on why you use them. If they are used superstitiously (as a kind of spell that magically gives your prayer some extra zing), they had better be dropped.

Why are they used at all?

They should make you aware of two things. In using them you are reminding yourself of the grounds for your right to enter God's presence. You would have no right to approach God the Father if it were not through the redeeming work of God the Son. It is wise to use the words, from time to time at least, so that you remember this.

The words are also used when making requests. Jesus himself made it clear that requests "in my name" would never be refused by the Father (Jn. 14:13-14). A request made "in the name of" Jesus, means a request that he authorizes. Jesus gave his followers authority to draw checks on the power bank of heaven. Clearly, however, the checks may only be drawn when the purpose of the check conforms with heavenly policy. It is only when I am acting as Christ's agent that I may pray "in his name."

I am the president of a certain provincial association. Along with the treasurer I have authority to sign checks *in the name of* the association. The bank will honor my checks when they are so drawn up and signed by me. It would even be possible for me to cash association checks for my personal pleasures. Possible—but wrong.

In the case of heaven's bank, prayers that terminate with the words "in the name of Jesus" but that do not reflect the will of Jesus, will not be honored. Heaven can spot what an earthly teller cannot.

Rightly understood, then, the expression "in the name of Jesus" can be an effective guard against praying drivel. Remember that prayer consists of collaborating with God in his divine purposes. If the words we are discussing remind you of this and cause you to weigh your requests carefully before making them, they serve a valuable purpose.

Have I any right to ask the Father to help me get an A on my term paper "in the name of Jesus"? It depends what my term paper has to do with his purposes. The apparent triviality of my request has no bearing on the problem. The fact that my term paper will mean nothing twenty years from now is irrelevant. To dry a single tear can be entirely within God's eternal purposes. What matters is whether my request conforms to his will.

But how can I know this?

We will talk later about knowing God's will in the chapter on guidance. For the present the following principles will help:

1. It is always God's will that we praise him, thank him and confess our sins.

2. It is always God's will that we be open with him about the longings of our heart. It is perfectly legitimate to tell him "Lord, I'd really like to get an A on my paper. It means a lot to me." He likes us to share with him (Ps. 103:13) even though he may not always give us what we want.

3. It is always God's will that we pray for our enemies (Mt. 5:44).

4. The more we learn about the Bible, the more we shall understand what God's view of things is. The more we understand about his outlook, the more we shall know what his will is in a given instance.

5. There are specific promises in the Bible. It is always God's will that when we pray, we take these promises seriously and count on their fulfillment.

6. When we are puzzled about what God's will *might* be, we are encouraged to ask for wisdom. We should do so with complete confidence that we will be given the understanding we need (Jas. 1:5-7).

The word *amen* is used too often as a habit. In conventional prayer it tells you when the prayer has ended. Through long custom it has become a verbalized period.

In the Bible amen has various meanings and could be translated "truth," "truly" or "so be it" according to the context. When Jesus used to say "verily, verily" the Greek term employed is a transliteration of the Hebrew word *amen*.

The most dramatic amens are found in the Book of Revelation, usually following a chorus of praise to God and the Lamb. In those instances the beings surrounding the throne express their hearty approval of the praises by using amen to mean something like, "Yes, O Lord, that is absolutely right!"

Perhaps this is the most appropriate way to use the word today. You will find that in the less inhibited prayer meetings people will signify their agreement with what someone else is praying by saying, "*Amen*, Lord! *Amen*!" Others will say, "Yes, Lord! Yes!" Since God is fluent in Hebrew and English, he probably doesn't mind which language is used and is glad that his children are united in their prayers.

Ought we to drop the amen at the end of prayers? Certainly, if it is used to mean "end of paragraph" or "prayer now over," then the answer is yes. But there are occasions when it is appropriate.

For instance, to request something "in the name of Jesus. Amen!" means "*let this be so* in this name of Jesus." Of course one might just as well say it in English as in Hebrew.

There is no magic in the Hebrew tongue. The point is that using the words "let this be so" reminds the person praying of the solemnity and the definiteness of the petition he is making. It says, "I am not just talking into thin air. This is a real request. Let it become reality."

Another occasion when it might be appropriate is when you make a positive affirmation of praise in prayer. At the end of the Lord's prayer, for instance, are the words "For Thine is the kingdom, the power, and the glory, for ever and ever. *And that's absolutely true, and I affirm it.*" (For that is what Amen means in that context.)

Whether you say your amens in English or in Hebrew is entirely up to you. So long as your inner eyes are turned upon the God of heaven, the language you employ will be relatively unimportant. But when praying with others sometimes there is value in conforming to their customs, provided you do not feel too unnatural in doing so.

Praying in Public
You will probably find it deeply rewarding to join other Christians in prayer. In our society when Christians meet for prayer, they usually pray one at a time. In this way everyone can participate in everyone else's prayer.

You may find yourself inhibited at first. Some Christians display verbal expertise in prayer. Some can use *thee* and *thou* fluently and with the correct verbs. Others are experts in "conversational prayer" and you may be unsure when they're through—because they don't say, "Amen." Any form of prayer (conversational or conventional) can be an exercise in eloquence, a piece of subtle showmanship or a sincere prayer. It can also be intimidating to the un-initiated.

Try praying with one Christian friend to start off. Then when you go to a larger prayer session, concentrate your thoughts on the God to whom you are all praying and not on the people who pray. It matters little what others think of your prayer. God wants to hear it. And *he* wants others to share it. If you can keep God in the center of your thoughts, you will be less likely to view public prayer as a performance.

Don't worry about your voice sounding shaky or squeaky. Just go ahead and talk to God. He will be delighted to hear your words, and new links of fellowship will be forged with the other Christians around you. Some of them will be given courage to pray because you prayed. Others will be glad about the subject of your prayer and echo it fervently in their hearts.

Hearing God's Voice

So far I have been evading the issue of how you hear God speaking when you pray. Jesus said, "My sheep hear my voice . . . and they follow me" (Jn. 10:27). How do you distinguish between your own thoughts or wishes and the voice of the Shepherd? Isn't it very easy to fool yourself? Worse still, isn't it possible to mistake evil voices for the voice of the Shepherd?

Let me get back to my basic point. It is God who wishes to establish communication. He is more anxious to speak to us than we are to hear him. He is incredibly persistent in trying to get through. Our real problem is that we tend to *avoid* hearing him.

Difficulties arise. First, let me say that when Jesus said "My sheep hear my voice," he was saying something a little different from what we commonly read into the verse. Our first impression is that he is telling us that from somewhere within us promptings will come, promptings accompanied by an infallible knowledge that Jesus is their origin. That is not exactly what he was saying.

To hear, in the Bible, usually carries the connotation of to *pay heed to*. Thus a follower of Jesus is someone who takes

God's injunctions seriously. He is distinguished from other "sheep" by the fact that he is determined to follow only the true Shepherd. When other voices clamor for his attention, he deliberately closes his ears to them. Only one voice will be obeyed.

And because he is determined to obey one voice alone, he will learn to distinguish that voice from others (Jn. 7:17). It may take time for him to do so. After all, lambs do not at first distinguish the Shepherd's voice, only the voice of the ewe.

In practical terms this means that as a Christian matures and increases in his understanding of divine things, he will become increasingly able to spot truth and distinguish it from error. It also means that his capacity to do so will be proportionate to his determination to obey his Lord.

But does not God also speak directly so that we have precise guidance with precise problems? Of course he does; and we shall deal with the matter more fully when we come to the topic of guidance. However God's main concern is to communicate *moral* guidance to us and to speak to us about right, wrong and how to relate to himself. And it is in this area that we should consider the use of the Bible in prayer.

The Bible and Prayer
Experienced pray-ers like to have a Bible handy when they pray. Some commence prayer with a reading from *Daily Light* (a collection of verses of Scripture grouped around a daily theme). Others read Scripture systematically.

Since I will discuss Bible study more fully in the next chapter, I shall limit myself here to dealing with negative points. There are dangers in using the Bible (or books like *Daily Light*). Many Christians I know look on their Bibles as horoscopes. They approach them armed with specific worries and hope that God will "speak" to them from their daily reading of Scripture.

The tragedy of this approach is that when you adopt it, you tend to miss the real teaching of a passage, screening it out through the filter of your own hopes and fears. You distort and twist the passage to make it fit like a poultice over your spiritual boils.

Now God sometimes will take a passage and with peculiar directness speak to you about a problem in your life. Remember, he is the One who wishes to communicate and who can use many ways of doing so. But for you to come to his Word insisting that it say *what you want it to say* is to close your ears to what God may really be telling you.

If you have a problem then, by all means unburden yourself before God. Leave the matter confidently with him. And as you turn to the Scriptures, put your problem out of your mind and (unless the passage is clearly and obviously addressing itself to the problem) seek to find what God is really saying in the passage.

Daydreaming
From time to time you will find your thoughts straying far away from God and prayer. This can be disconcerting and discouraging.

When my thoughts wandered I used to say, "Oh, I'm sorry Lord, I wish I didn't wander like this. Please help me not to . . . " and then off I would go into another daydream.

The causes of daydreams are many, tiredness being the most common. I know no way of avoiding them, but it is important to react rightly when you realize what you are doing.

What is it, do you think, that brings you back to the point? Or better still, who is it? When I discover myself daydreaming, my response now is, "Thank you, Lord. Thank you for rescuing me again. I would waste a lot more time daydreaming if it weren't for you." I don't grovel. I don't waste time in bitter self-recrimination or in discouragement. I rejoice in the infinite patience of God who never gives up and who calls me constantly back to himself.

The Practice of the Presence

It is good to have a set time to meet with God daily. But it becomes a bad thing if you feel that communion is confined to that brief period. Meister Eckhart, an old mystic, urged Christians to carry from their secret meeting with God "the same frame of mind" into the world around them. You see, you do not leave God when you go from the quiet place any more than he leaves you. A "quiet time" is a "tuning in" time. You should not switch off the radio once you have tuned in to God's wavelength. Thomas Kelly in his book *Testament of Devotion* talks about living on two planes at once. Impossible as it may seem, it is the unusual privilege of the Christian to be aware of God at all times. Brother Lawrence in the little book *The Practice of the Presence of God* speaks simply and straight-forwardly of the same thing.

You need not constantly be formulating verbal petitions, but like the psalmist you may enjoy the Lord "always before your face." It may be that such a practice is what Paul refers to when he urges us to "Pray constantly" (1 Thess. 5:17). You may leave the room where you pray, but you do not have to leave the inner sanctuary deep inside your being.

Still, old habits of mind may be hard to overcome. Most of the time, whether we are aware of it or not, our minds are occupied at the same time with the intellectual tasks on hand or the impression we think we are making on those around us or how much time we have or a hundred other things. "Pure concentration" on one task is almost impossible. Our minds function simultaneously on various levels even when we are concentrating hard on a mathematical problem. The capacity to carry out our tasks efficiently while we continue to praise God presents no difficulty as far as our brain function is concerned. Our difficulty is simply that old habits of thought want to reassert themselves and crowd out what is most needed.

The Holy Spirit wishes to make us more aware of God at all times. Just as we wander in thought when having devotions, we will constantly wander in thought all day long. And each time we become aware of doing so, it is because God is getting through to us again. Don't waste time kicking yourself when you wake up to the fact that your thoughts have been anywhere but where they should be. Immediately say, "Thank you, Lord. Thank you because you never cease to speak to me. Thank you that you are always near."

Summary
In this chapter we have learned that God constantly seeks communion with us. Prayer consists of responding to God. We should set aside a period every day specifically for prayer. During that time we should give ourselves to worship and thanksgiving, to confession, to fellowship and to petitions and intercession. No special form is needed, but the Spirit will teach us reverence as we wait on God. As we leave our formal quiet time, we should let God teach us the secret of remaining in his presence throughout the day.

A Few Suggestions
A. Passages to use in praise and worship. (Try singing them to music you make up as you go along.)
    Psalm 92:1-5
    Psalm 93:1-5
    Psalm 95:1-11
    Psalm 96:1-13
    Psalm 97:1-12
    Psalm 100:1-5
    Psalm 103:1-22
B. Books to read.
    Prayer, Hallesby.

The Practice of the Presence of God, Brother Lawrence.
A Testament of Devotion, Thomas Kelly.
C. A Commitment to consider.

"And in the morning, a great while before day, he rose and went out to a lonely place, and there he prayed." Mark 1:35

"In these days he went out into the hills to pray; and all night he continued in prayer to God." Luke 6:12

I resolve, by the help of God, to set aside at least twenty minutes every day to spend alone in God's presence.

Signed_____

Date_____

3

God Still Speaks

They seemed an unlikely bunch. I was sure they were bona fide Christians. I had led them to Christ myself. Yet just as I would be feeling reassured that they were turning out well, they would do and say the strangest things. I clucked over them like a nervous hen worried lest I had hatched swans.

We were all students in the same residence hall. Somehow they did not conform to my stereotype of a Christian. Not that conforming to a stereotype was important, but they just didn't seem to be "tuned in."

Yet one year later I had no hesitation in calling them godly. They knew what they believed and knew where they were going in life. They had become Christians. The only way I can account for the difference was that during the intervening months we all had been studying Scripture steadily, both individually and collectively.

Pat, a six-foot, genial athlete, was another guy who had me worried. Friendly, helpful, but clueless. On impulse I loaned him a book about daily Bible study and never saw him again for six months.

When we ran across each other later I was astounded. Same face. Same build. Different man.

I had forgotten about the book but Pat hadn't. "It changed my life," he told me seriously, "at least, daily, prayerful Bible study did." It was not the sort of language he would have used six months before.

Pat has now been a missionary for many years. I need not have been surprised. Scripture claims to have profound effects on us. "Like newborn babes," writes Peter, "desire the sincere milk of the word, *that ye may grow thereby*" (1 Pet. 2:2).

In chapter one I pointed out that the very life of God was planted within you when you became a Christian. You were born again. I also pointed out that spiritual life, like biological life, has its own developmental needs, one of which is truth. As you absorb truth from Scripture, spiritual life will thrive within you. As Peter says, you will grow as you feed on the milk of the Word.

Scripture truth is more than milk, however. It varies in texture and substance, and correspondingly in ease of digestion. The more you develop spiritually the better able you will be to stomach the "meat" of Scripture. Strong truth makes strong Christians stronger.

Scripture also gives you clear moral guidelines to live by. They will not always be in the form of simple do's and don'ts. God designed Scripture to give moral orientation to people living in any culture, in any age and in any moral climate.

Your sense of right and wrong (call it "conscience" or "superego" or whatever) was developed by your upbringing and by other moral influences surrounding you. If you were reared by parents who were strong-minded teetotalers, you will feel uneasy if you start to drink irrespective of the real morality of drinking. People in some savage tribes kill under certain circumstances with a feeling of doing a virtuous thing. Few people in North America would feel the same way. You may even have questioned whether absolute rights and wrongs exist.

They do. God himself is the absolute standard, and while such matters as motive and local custom are of great importance, there are moral absolutes in the very structure of the universe. But how do you find them? How can consciences be reoriented?

Scripture sheds light on morality because it reveals God himself. Study it with a willingness to pay the cost of obedience, and order will gradually replace confusion. "How can a young man keep his way pure? By guarding it according to thy word" (Ps. 119:9).

But Scripture will do more. Truth liberates. It not only reveals a standard but will set you free to keep it. This is what makes Scripture so different from other ethical systems, which are powerless to help the struggler. You may not experience Scripture's full effect at once, but as time goes on it will become increasingly influential in shaping your behavior. "I have laid up thy word in my heart, that I might not sin against thee" (Ps. 119:11).

The change will not be without conflict. There is a personal devil. Habit will be on his side as he actively opposes your attempts to live as God would have you live. I shall talk more about the subject later, but for the present you should notice that the weapon most effective in countering his attacks according to St. Paul is "the sword of the Spirit, which is the word of God" (Eph. 6:17). A knowledge of Scripture is invaluable when you encounter the power of darkness.

There are other things Scripture will do for you. It will make you wise: wiser than people around you; wiser than your professors. Notice, I said *wiser,* not more knowledgeable. A wise man is one who can distinguish what is fundamental from what is trivial, who knows what life is about and who acts appropriately whatever the circumstances.

In the university there are many people who can impress us with incomprehensible twaddle. There are also brilliant men. But there are few wise men. "I have more understanding than all my teachers," wrote a psalmist long ago, "for thy testimonies are my meditation. I understand more than the aged, for I keep thy precepts" (Ps. 119:99-100).

Wisdom, you must understand, is always humble and open to learn. The wisdom that God gives through Scripture does not lead you to quote a Bible verse to contradict a biology professor's assertions. Such actions spring from bigotry and naiveté rather than godly wisdom.

Later on I speak of guidance in a Christian's life and about what part Scripture plays in it. The same psalmist I have already quoted wrote, "Thy word is a lamp to my feet and a light to my path." (Ps. 119:105). However, he was talking about a *moral* pathway rather than a geographic one. The only comment I want to make here is the same one I made in discussing prayer. The Bible is not a horoscope. Never try to read into Scripture mysterious instructions about your daily activities.

Neither is the Bible a sedative. It does not tranquilize. Yet in reading it you will find peace. "Great peace have those who love thy law" (Ps. 119:165). Chemical tranquilizing agents can work by blunting the impact reality has on you. Scripture does not. It imparts peace by showing you how to resolve any inner conflicts that destroy peace.

Peace is more than the absence of anxiety. It is a positive quality arising from inner harmony. A peace which is destroyed by external threats is no peace. God's peace, which will grow the more you understand Scripture, defies uncertainty and danger. It is the clear-eyed peace with which the Roman Christians faced hungry lions in ancient arenas and with which Eastern European Christians now face imprisonment, torture and threats to their families. It is a peace which comes from the understanding that God is in charge, that you belong to him, and that chaos and uncertainty around you represent only the confusing surface of reality.

And such peace, understandably, improves your physical well-being. It is "marrow to your bones."

Practical Problems
I could continue to list the benefits of regular Scripture reading, but why should I? The living God has spoken. The ruler of the universe has revealed himself in print. Yet still we hesitate. Why?

You may, of course, have doubts that the Bible is inspired by God. You may feel uncomfortable precisely because you are supposed to approach it with reverence or with a special set of feelings which you cannot produce because of your inner doubts.

The best way to deal with those inner doubts is to expose yourself to the Bible. Don't approach it with any special feelings, except for a willingness to put into practice any truth you see in it. I could argue about inspiration, but I refuse to. Find out for yourself. The least we can say about the Bible is that it is a compilation of historical documents whose validity (as historical data) is now above reproach. Read it and let it speak to you. Pray, "Please show me, O God, if these documents *do* constitute your Word." But read openly. Try to understand what is actually being said. Be willing to incorporate whatever truth you see into your own life.

"Ah, you have me there," a research scientist once confessed to me thoughtfully. "I'm not sure I can take the risk. It might mean leaving my job and being a missionary or something." He was not joking. Few people are quite so honest, and I could offer him no guarantees as to what demands might be made of him.

On the other hand your problem may be the very opposite. You may be *too* conscious of the Bible's unique character—so conscious, in fact, that you are inhibited when you read.

Many years ago in Latin America I was astonished to discover that Roman Catholic students (who in those days had had little or no exposure to Scripture) and communist students were far better at Bible study than students from evangelical churches. In group study the communists and Catholics were quick to see what the passage *actually said.* Many evangelical students, on the other hand, had a mental block at this point. They seemed only able to see what the Bible *was supposed to say.* It was as though they screened Bible statements through a doctrinal filter, seeing that which they had been trained to expect. ("It can't say *that* because the Bible doesn't teach that.")

Or maybe you expect some kind of magic. I think that was my problem years ago in my chilly early morning experiments. I had a preconceived notion as to *how* God would speak from Scripture. When what I expected did not take place, I was confused and disappointed.

Scripture is not magic. It is truth expressed in words, sentences and paragraphs. (The verse numbers and chapter headings are artificial and were imposed by translators long after the original documents were compiled.)

But someone will object, "Isn't it true that the Bible can only be understood when the Holy Spirit opens our understanding and speaks to us from it?" Quite so. But the question almost implies that the Holy Spirit needs to be persuaded. It seems to suggest that before he can speak, you have to go through a special "tuning in" session or that the words themselves are difficult and obscure, so that only if you are in some specially inspired condition, can obscurity be resolved into profundity.

God's desire is to make matters plain to anyone, anytime, anywhere. In addition to providing us with documents that are for the most part simply and clearly written, he quickens our minds by his Spirit, provided we genuinely want to know. Pride, prejudice and preconceptions are the big barriers to seeing truth. Be humble. Look at what is there. Tell God you know your mind has limitations. Thank him that he will help you understand.

Of course we use the word "understand" in two ways. Sometimes when we say, "I don't understand," we mean, "I can't grasp what the writer is trying to say." At other times we mean, "I can see what he's saying all right, but I don't see how it could be true."

Both types of problem can arise when you read Scripture. The problem of the words not making sense often resolves itself when you use a modern translation. There are many such translations and I will discuss them later. The second kind of problem ("I see what it says, but I can't believe it's true") is a sign that you are thinking about what you are reading. People who never hit problems of this sort are only going through the motions of reading.

The first thing to do is to make sure you *have* read the passage correctly. You may be puzzling over something it didn't say in the first place. But if having checked you are still shaking your head, there are many steps you can take.

You are not likely to be the first person to be puzzled. Chances are that many people have already wrestled with the same problem. Some of their thoughts will be recorded in Bible commentaries. (We'll talk about these later too.) You may be puzzled simply because the Scripture conflicts with your prior ideas about what the Bible *ought* to say. But in any case, remember that in learning about the most profound mysteries of being, you are likely to come across ideas that shake and disturb you. Some will be gateways to profound insights. Others will continue to puzzle you. If they do, don't stop learning, but file the puzzle in the "unsolved" compartment of your mind, having committed the matter to God in prayer. Five years from now you may not understand what it was that bothered you.

How to Study

There are several ways to study the Bible. I hope you will eventually use all of them, but to start with one or two will be sufficient. None of the methods can be divided rigidly from any other. Their boundaries overlap. Each, when used properly, tends to check the weaknesses of the others.

You can study the Bible devotionally. By this I mean that during the regular time of quiet you spend with God each day, you can meditate prayerfully on a few verses of Scripture. Whatever other form of study you adopt, do adopt this one.

It is best to follow some regular plan (like *This Morning with God* or *Scripture Union Notes*). Devotional reading does not mean you must switch your intellect off. It simply means your emphasis should be that of a personal application, in a spirit of reverence, of what you read.

I had my own little scheme years ago. In a pocket notebook I would make a quick note of whatever helpful lesson arose from the passage. In the margin of my Bible I would jot down the reference next to the verse that had spoken to me. "B65" would mean that my comment on the verse could be found in notebook B, page 65. As I went through the Bible several times some verses would have several references beside them, as fresh insights came. Having to jot something down kept me on my toes and helped me avoid mental laziness. It also forced me to clarify hazy insights.

Devotional Bible study is helpful if there are questions in your mind as you read such as:

Is there a warning for me here?
Is there a promise I can claim?
Is there an example for me to follow?
Are there commands I must obey?
Is there a sin I must avoid or confess?
Is there some encouragement I can take to heart?

Is there some new lesson about God I can thank him for?
Are there words of praise I can echo?
Is there an experience described that has been true of
me?

The disadvantage of confining Bible study to devotional
study is that it offers an unbalanced diet—too much milk,
too little meat. It needs to be supplemented by other forms.

You can study a whole book of the Bible inductively. Inductive
study is the kind where you look at a whole book in an attempt to find the basic principles it demonstrates. You ask
such questions as, "What are the main points the writer is
making? How can I express them in my own words?"

Inductive and deductive reasoning are complementary.
You need both in any discipline. Too many students confine their approach to the Bible to a deductive one, saying
"Since A and B are true, then according to my rule the book
should say X and Y." With deductive reasoning you begin
with a rule, and test the material by your rule. Inductive
reasoning on the other hand looks at the material to try to
find *what rules arise from it.* As both kinds of reasoning have
been used in understanding the Scripture, Bible students
have been amazed at the unity and consistency of its teaching. But beginners should start with an inductive approach.

Inductive Bible study lays the groundwork for systematic
study. It can be carried out alone or with a group of people
who agree to study the same book and who can check one
another's thinking. Many books have been written to teach
you the principles of this kind of study, and I list some at
the end of the chapter.

I have very strong feelings about inductive Bible study
and I plan to amplify them at the end. Skip anything you
like in this chapter, but do read the last few pages.

You can also read the Bible through from beginning to end.
This is a less formidable task than you might suppose. G.
Campbell Morgan once read the whole Bible through

aloud and at pulpit speed in 96 hours. If you read four chapters a day you will cover the material in about nine months.

There are advantages in this sort of reading. You get a "bird's eye" view of a wide variety of biblical writings over a period of 1600 years. You also pick up the astonishing interrelatedness of the various parts of Scripture—particularly of the Old and New Testaments. Many of the passages will become treasures as you discover them yourself for the first time. Other passages you may have to wade through.

Use a modern translation for this sort of reading. Try it as a bedtime snack.

You can also study the Bible systematically or doctrinally. By this I mean you trace a given idea through the whole Bible. You might also want to compare what you find with what scholars down the ages have written.

This is by far the toughest form of study, and to my way of thinking it should not be tackled until one has a mastery of the other three methods (though many Bible teachers begin by instructing new converts in this method).

Again there are a number of books which are helps in beginning this type of study, and I mention them also at the end of the chapter.

Translations and Paraphrases
(Skip this section if you find it boring and go on to p. 51.)

While some Christians have to make do with only one version of Scripture in their language, and others with none at all, English speaking Christians face a bewildering variety of translations and versions. You can learn the history of the main Catholic and Protestant translations elsewhere. Here I will give only a general guide written from a personal point of view.

One can divide Bible translations in print at the moment

into the following major categories for our discussion here:

Older translations

Revisions

Personal translations

Paraphrases

New translations

Translations with editorial notes and comments

The principal Protestant *older translation* is still the King James or Authorized Version. The structure of the seventeenth-century English is sonorous and beautiful. Many words have changed their meaning since the version came out. In addition there are minor errors in translation. It is worthwhile to own a copy since much Christian preaching and literature refers to this version.

Scholars have produced three different updated *revisions* of the older Authorized Version. The first, produced by British scholars in the 1880s, is known as the Revised Version. Earlier this century, North American scholars produced the American Standard Version and later the Revised Standard Version (the most readable of the three). All of these revisions are revisions of the original "King James" translation. They were all conducted by groups of scholars, working as teams.

By *personal translations* I mean translations made by an individual scholar. There are many of these, one of the liveliest and most popular being the translation of the New Testament by J. B. Phillips, though many people regard Phillips' New Testament as a paraphrase rather than a true translation. Individual translations vary in quality with the personal biases and skill of the translator. They can have the advantage of being delightfully fresh. They can have the disadvantage of less accuracy and a more idiosyncratic bias.

Paraphrases tend to sacrifice precision in translation in the interest of intelligibility. They (for example, The Living

Bible) are less meticulous about exactness in translation than about English semantics. They have advantage for readability but disadvantage for more careful study. The author of the paraphrase tells you what he thinks the verse means in lucid contemporary idiom. He interprets as well as translates. He knows a lot more than most of us do, so his views are to be respected. But his work should be compared with more careful translations.

The *expanded paraphrase* can be misleading unless you really understand what it is about. Most translations try to choose the exact meaning of a particular word by the context, for contexts change the meanings of words. They therefore select one of several possible meanings. The writer of an expanded paraphrase on the other hand will tell you all the possible meanings of a given word or phrase.

Words may be used metaphorically or literally, and only the context will tell us which. For instance the following two sentences will conjure up different images in your mind.

1. He plunged into the raging torrent.
2. He plunged into his work.

An expanded paraphrase might translate sentence 2 as follows: He plunged (flung himself into, dived, threw himself bodily, leapt, jumped head first submerging himself, by a sudden action immersed his whole body) into his work (toil, labor).

The expanded paraphrase leaves you to select whichever alternative attracts you the most. If you are anything like the rest of us, you will choose either the most dramatic alternative or the alternative which fits in best with certain prejudices you have. However, your choice will not necessarily reflect what the writer wanted to say. The expanded paraphrase is a "pick whichever meaning you prefer" version. It creates the illusion of giving a "deeper" meaning by a semantic trick. It focuses too much on individual words.

New translations do not attempt to update older ones. They start from scratch. Since they are more recent than some of the revisions, their authors also have access to more early documents and fragments. The New English Bible is a new translation.

Versions with notes. Catholics and protestants alike have published versions of Scripture designed to promote a particular theological viewpoint by incorporating footnotes along with the text. Such versions should generally be avoided not because of the view they promote but because of the mental and spiritual laziness they produce. Once you have heard an expert tell you what a passage means, you will find it easier to accept his opinion than to think one out for yourself. This is bad since the teachings that really stick with you are those you worked out for yourself. You will say, "Who am I to differ with an expert?" Good question. I hope to answer it partly as I conclude this chapter. But before I do so, let me remind you that even experts differ. Things are not true simply because they get into print, even if the print is on the same paper as Holy Writ.

The Time Factor

"How can I find time to do all this Bible study? Christ promised to give me rest, yet it seems all he does is to load me with extra assignments."

Not really. It is not Christ who overloads us with assignments. We overload ourselves. We perpetually take on more than we can do, then complain we are overworked. Among the things we load ourselves with are some that are good but not essential and many that are trivial and meaningless. Life becomes simpler when we wise up to the fact that we do not need to busy ourselves with two-thirds of our daily activities. Life stripped to its essentials is freedom.

And for the Christian, serious Bible study is an essential. Get rid of some nonessentials in your life and set aside a regular, weekly three-hour period for serious Bible study in addition to your daily reading.

You find time to eat, to sleep, to wash and to work. Some people also find time to attend a weekly movie or to spend hours playing games, watching TV, practicing hobbies, playing instruments, socializing, reading garbage. Find time to study the Bible whatever else you may have to drop.

But how do I proceed? Let's say I free up three hours a week to study the Bible. What do I do then?

First you make sure that you have proper study materials. To start you will need:

A King James Bible (or New Testament)

A modern translation of the Bible (or New Testament)

A looseleaf notebook.

In addition it will be helpful to buy one or both of the following:

The New Bible Commentary

The New Bible Dictionary.

Where shall I begin to study? You must decide on a book to study. If you are a new Christian, I suggest that you start with Luke's Gospel. I feel that to start with *one* of the four Gospels is a must. The Gospel of John was written to convince non-Christians of Christ's deity. For that reason, while it may be good to study John, my suggestion would be to begin with one of the other three.

Each of these three Gospels has points in its favor. The value of all of them is that they serve to emphasize Christianity as an historical faith. It stands or falls on events that took place in time and space. Supremely it is centered in the life, teachings, death and resurrection of the God-man who entered time-space via the uterus of a peasant woman two thousand years ago.

Luke's Gospel, more than any other, is preoccupied with the problem of sifting and analyzing all the reports surrounding the birth, life, death and resurrection of Jesus, and with recording as accurate an account of them as possible. For this reason I recommend it as a starting point for your serious study. But if you have other convictions about other books in the Bible which you want to get at first, please remember I am only suggesting.

Having collected my notebook, Bibles and my commentaries, how do I proceed? Well, if you're a serious student in other subjects, I really shouldn't have to tell you. While no real understanding of Scripture is possible apart from the Holy Spirit, the *techniques* of Bible study differ from no other textual study. But to refocus your thinking, let me remind you that your object in any textual study is:

1. to see exactly what the text says,

2. to decide what the text means, and

3. to explore the relevance of the text to contemporary life generally and to your own life in particular.

This being so you must understand the contexts. First, you must understand the context of the whole book. By reading either the introduction to the book in the *New Bible Commentary* or the entry discussing the book in the *New Bible Dictionary* you will learn something about the time the book was written, contemporary concerns and problems, something about the authorship, plus problems and discussions that have preoccupied previous students of the book. But only read the detailed analysis of the book in the commentary *after* your personal study of the text.

You should write brief notes from your reading to summarize what you see as important from this to clarify your grasp of the *contextual climate* surrounding the whole book.

Then you should read right through the book—not just once, but several times. Don't read with a blank mind. Read probing for answers to questions. What is the writer's purpose in writing? Why does he record the incidents he does? Is there any plan to the book, or is it written haphazardly? Can it be divided into sections, and if so can titles be given to the sections? Are there any themes running through the book from beginning to end, like a leitmotif in a piece of music?

When you are able to answer these questions add a further introductory section to your notes. Try at the same time to write down a very simple outline of what *you* see as its main sections and where they begin and end.

You will then be in a position to examine each section in detail for you will have begun to understand the general context in which each paragraph, each sentence, each word is found. And as you do so you will keep in mind the same three basic questions: What does the passage actually say? What does it mean? How does it apply here and now? Never tackle the third question before you have answered the second. Discipline yourself fiercely never to answer the second question until you have looked the first one squarely in the face.

I need say no more for now. Many, many helpful books have been written on this whole subject. I only wish to let a wild, warm enthusiasm flow from my heart down my arm to flood from my pen on to the paper. Bible study has torn apart my life and remade it. That is to say that God, through his Word, has done so. In the darkest periods of my life when everything seemed hopeless, I would struggle in the grey dawns of many faraway countries to grasp the basic truths of Scripture passages. I looked for no immediate answers to my problems. Only did I sense intuitively that I was drinking drafts from a fountain that gave life to my soul.

Slowly as I grappled with textual and theological problems, a strength grew deep within me. Foundations cemented themselves to an other-worldly rock beyond the reach of time and space, and I became strong and more alive. If I could write poetry about it I would. If I could sing through paper, I would flood your soul with the glorious melodies that express what I have found. I cannot exaggerate for there are no expressions majestic enough to tell of the glory I have seen or of the wonder of finding that I, a neurotic, unstable, middle-aged man have my feet firmly planted in eternity and breathe the air of heaven. And all this has come to me through a careful study of Scripture.

Setting a Goal

For in this study I have experienced an ever deepening knowledge of a person. We talk about *knowing* but in two different senses. I can know facts. But I can also know people. Knowing facts is intellectual process. Knowing people involves emotional and volitional interactions with them.

You may read the Bible to know certain facts. But this is only the beginning. Your real aim is to know Christ. You must therefore set yourself, as you study Scripture, to get to know a person.

There are many experts on the Bible. Some will awe you by the facility with which they quote chapter and verse. Others will hint at a knowledge of the original languages. You will come across people with a formidable fund of information on any passage you could name, ready to expatiate on the subtler nuances of the biblical text at the drop of a hat.

Don't mimic them.

Knowledge, especially biblical knowledge has the same effect as wine when it goes to your head. You become dizzily exalted. But Bible study should be conducted not with a view to *knowing about* Christ but to *knowing him* personally.

And to know Christ is to know peace. The more you know him, the less inclined you will be to impress people or to indulge in games of biblical one-upmanship. The Bible was inspired because God wants you to know him. He wants to reveal his heart to you in a love relationship. If you let him, he will make that relationship so precious

that it will become a private thing that you will want to share
with no one. You may be willing enough to talk about *him*.
You will be glad to tell others of his goodness. But there
will be secret issues between you that are between you and
him alone. And he will make your life as stable as a rock and
as alive as spring.

Beyond the sacred page
I seek Thee, Lord,
My spirit pants for Thee,
O living Word.[1]

A Few Suggestions
A. Aids to Bible study.

1. *The New Bible Commentary*: A one-volume commentary. Helpful provided you attempt to come to grips with
the passage *before* you examine the commentary's analysis
of the biblical text itself.

2. *The New Bible Dictionary*: A superb tool for Bible study
—really an encyclopedia on any topic in the Bible. Included
are entries giving background on every book in the Bible.

3. *This Morning with God*: Four volumes helpful for devotional Bible study. It prevents you from falling into haphaz-
ard daydreaming by giving penetrating questions and rele-
vant suggestions. It will take you through the entire Bible.

4. *Scripture Union Notes*: There is a broad range from
serious notes for advanced study to simple devotional ones
for young Christians. All have the same basic aim—to encourage profitable daily Bible study.

B. For your own "Quiet Time."

1. Read Psalm 19. As you read, make a note of the two
ways in which God has revealed himself to man.

2. Verses 1-6. It is sometimes suggested that it is impossible to know anything about God apart from Scripture.
What can be known from celestial bodies, and who can
know it?

3. Verses 7-10. The words *law, testimony, statutes* and so forth are all used synonymously here. Make a list of what they can do for you.

4. Verses 11-14. Try repeating these verses aloud and making them your own prayer.

4

On Being a Signpost

They could not have looked like promising revolutionary material. That they should see themselves as deliverers of Israel was ludicrous. Their grasp of the meaning of Christ's death and resurrection was still tenuous and their perception of their future confused.

What was going to happen on the political scene? What role would they play? Seated among the young olive trees they asked him: "Do you plan to restore Israel's sovereignty?" Many eyes were turned on him.

"None of your business" was the effect of his retort. "That's God the Father's affair. He currently organizes the political scene. Your job will be to bear witness to me not only here, but in broadening circles throughout the earth" (see Acts 1:4-8).

Was he out of his mind? Who would believe them? What credibility would this unsophisticated group of petty misfits have in the cynical world? How much impact could they make on its tough, hostile shell?

"The Holy Ghost will come upon you...."

And so it happened. Within a decade Jerusalem had

been rocked to her foundations, and cities around the Mediterranean basin from Jerusalem to Rome had been stirred by feeble followers of Jesus. All the new Christians were witnesses. A few became full-fledged evangelists gifted in presenting the good news with convincing clarity and power. The two (witnesses and evangelists) worked hand in hand in the church's task of making disciples among all nations.

Today the situation remains unchanged. Every member of the worldwide church is a witness while some have special gifts in evangelism, pastoral care and so on.

And like the witness in court you are obliged to tell the truth, the whole truth and nothing but the truth. You will tell the truth in the sense that you are to tell what actually happened to you rather than a dressed up version of what happened to you. You need neither exaggerate nor minimize what has taken place in your life or what is currently taking place. You will tell the whole truth in the sense that when there is an opportunity you will not hold anything back. You will be prepared to let your life be an open book read by all the people around you.

You will give up your right to be a "private person." Just as Christ was ready to share all that he was with everyone he countered, so you will be ready to share all that he has made you with anyone you meet. You will not ram your views down anybody's throat. You will simply be open and share.

You will not only share the triumphs you have experienced but the doubts, the fears and the defeats. To do anything less would be to act as an untruthful witness. You have nothing to hide. The truth itself is infinitely more powerful than the filtered version of the truth that your vanity might prefer.

I do not know whether or not God will give you the gift of being an evangelist. In the general teamwork of the church, evangelists (not just the big name ones but all men and women with a special gift for being used in the most crucial stages of God's rescue operation) have a limited role. All of us however have the broader responsibility of bearing witness.

The Nature of Signposts

And what does it mean to bear witness? Witnesses to what? Witnesses before whom? Is a witness something you *are*, something you *say* or something you *do*? Do you wait till someone asks you for your evidence or do you go right ahead whether they ask or not?

A witness of something you are, but what you are always determines what you say and do. The three—being, saying and doing—are part of a whole. Essentially a witness is someone *who is truthful about what he has seen, heard, or personally experienced.* Moreover the witness of Jesus must not only tell the truth but live it.

Two illustrations will serve to clarify. In a court of law a witness in response to questions tells the court what he heard, said or did. If he says, "I believe the prisoner was uptown that night because someone—I can't remember who it was—told me they'd seen him, . . ." his testimony will be ruled inadmissible. "Did you yourself see the prisoner downtown?" is what the court wants to know. It cannot deal with a witness's conjectures or on secondhand stories.

In the same way your Christian witness must be first-hand witness. It must be about what *you* discovered when *you* read the Bible, prayed, put *your* trust in Christ or whatever.

The second illustration of witness is that of a signpost. A signpost points to a destination. It matters little whether the signpost is pretty or ugly, old or new. It helps if the lettering is bold and clear. But the essential features are that it must point in the right direction and be clear about what it is pointing to.

If you ask people to describe the signposts that directed

them to their destination, they will remember some and forget others altogether. But forgotten or remembered, the signposts will have done their job if they have got the traveler to where he wanted to go.

"Ye shall be witnesses unto me," Jesus told the early disciples. In a sense it matters very little whether you are an antiqued rural signpost written in elegant ancient script or a bright green modern one strung up high over the freeway. You do not exist to draw attention to yourself but to direct people's thoughts to a divine destination. A signpost has defeated its purpose if it is so attractive that it draws attention to itself rather than to a city.

Therefore remember that in witnessing, while you will be talking about your personal experience, giving as it were a firsthand report of your encounter with Christ, your witness will not focus on you but on the Christ you experience. A newly engaged fellow or girl may talk about their engagement in one of two ways. One will give a self-centered account of conquest, of parties and be enamored more with the state of being engaged than with the person to whom he or she is engaged; another, while confessing his or her love, will speak in glowing terms of the person who has won them. Don't be enamored with the blessed state of being a Christian, but be enamored with Christ and confess what he means to you.

Unfortunately, witnessing is not seen by many Christians as a simple telling the truth or being a signpost. It has become a complex matter focusing at times on technicalities of witness and on irrelevancies.

Some people "witness" by carrying leatherbound Bibles, other by giving tracts to service station attendants or leaving literature in public toilets. Many sport bumper stickers ranging from the ancient fish symbol to "Honk if you love Jesus." Yet others erect roadside billboards. One sign near where I live reads, "The wicked will go to hell and burn forever." Some older postreformation groups witness by their dress. Amish and Mennonite men of certain groups do not wear ties or shave their beards, feeling it would be worldly to do so.

How can you know what true witness is? Does wearing no tie point people to Jesus? Do bumper stickers? Does bowing your head and saying grace in a restaurant?

Let me return to my original point. Witness is a pointing to Jesus—not to a religious movement or even to a way of life, but to a person. A witness is someone who tells others what he himself has personally and directly discovered about Jesus and God's Word. He is a signpost.

So long as we fall down in our open declaration of what we personally have experienced, bumper stickers are as pointless as such things as carrying a Bible "for a testimony," unusual forms of dress and so forth. In some cases the forms of "witness" I have mentioned become misleading and self-defeating. The signpost has drawn attention to itself rather than to Jesus. The fact that the more eccentric forms of Jesus-publicity give rise to derision in no way makes them Christian, however virtuous it makes the performer feel. The derision is not about Jesus but about our own kookiness. And while as kooks we may fancy ourselves persecuted for Jesus' sake, it would be more true to say that we are being laughed at because we are behaving ridiculously by man's standards as well as by God's.

But before we concentrate on technicalities and specifics, let us establish the absolute necessity of witness. If you are a new Christian, do not on any account be a secret one. The Christ who died for you demands that you confess your allegiance to him before your friends. Should you fail to do so, you will not only be acting in a manner unfaithful to Christ but will become the unhappy denizen of two worlds, feeling fully at home in neither. With your old friends you will find that the magic is gone, however hard you try to rekindle it. With your fellow Christians you will talk a "Christian" language, have a different set of jokes, shared clichés and ethical mores. With either group you may feel embarrassed when you are discovered in the company of the other.

It is not a matter of severing one set of relations in order to cement another but of being an honest person in both. The decision about what groups you belong to is not your decision. You belong to Christ. Belong to him openly and you will find that some people will reject you while others will be the more eager to welcome you.

Some people find it easy to be open. They call up their closest friends by telephone: "Listen, I've gotta talk to you. I've become a Christian. I went to this meeting, like.... And y'know for weeks I've been.... Listen, you must meet some of the guys...." The events in their lives are turned into exuberant testimony.

Others find it hard. They choke on words like "God" and "Jesus" and "Christian." They set out to say what they mean but beat around the bush; they use obscure words; their sentences meander in long meaningless tangles, like kitten-mauled wool.

Salesman for Christ?

How does one "witness"?

I cannot give you a technique. Other people might. But I don't know you. Nor do I know the people you bump into every day. Your Instructor is the Holy Spirit.

I can however tell you what constitutes bad witness. Bad witness is insincere witness, and though no one wants to be insincere, many approaches to and training courses in witness unwittingly pander to our phoniness.

For instance there are techniques based on the tacit assumption that Christ is a product for whom a market needs to be created. We must mass produce Christian packages and sell them. For some it is high pressure salesmanship with an urgency to clinch the deal. For others it is the soft sell of "friendship evangelism." ("I'm going to be nice to you so as to earn the right to plug Jesus to you.") No market needs to be created. The market is already there. The fields are white unto harvest. Salesmanship is both the glory and the shame of Western civilization. It has been its making and will ultimately prove its undoing.

The salesman projects an image. Ideally he should be a neat dresser, have white teeth, radiate good humor and ooze prosperity. Though he has a patter (learned and relearned in company conventions under the tutelage of genial sales "coaches"), he tries to be sincere by convincing first himself, and then you, that he is doing both you and society a kindness in offering you his company's product.

In the same way we market the Christ-package. We do it on TV and radio spots, magazine ads and above all through salesmen—salesmen who sell their product from pulpits and the army of lesser lights who market him part time from door-to-door or wherever they can.

It would be very wrong of me to suggest that this sort of thing is nothing more than a farce. What I am saying is that the church is in part a product of the Bible and in part of the Western free enterprise system.

Only if you understand this are you in a position to size up so many witnessing techniques. Like the salesman, the Christian is supposed to give a good impression. He should dress well "as a witness to Christ." He should smile. (Christians are supposed to be joyful.) He should be able, without losing his temper, to outtalk the non-Christian and corral him gently with words. He must beat him in sports, outperform him on the job and outshine him in brilliance. In all these ways Christians have unconsciously taken over a cultural rather than a biblical view of witness.

It is hard to do all those things—and many more—without being a phoney or living under an impossible strain. For instance you can't know everything. That being so, it is inevitable that when you talk about Christ, other people will raise points you have never thought of. They may do so just to be argumentative, or they may raise a genuine difficulty from their special knowledge or their own erroneous thinking in some area you are not familiar with.

At this point you have a choice of saying, "I'm sorry. I never thought of that. I don't know how to answer your question," or you can bluff it through in an evangelistic con game in order to keep the upper hand. And to do that is to be phoney.

Projecting a Christian image has pitfalls of its own. If I am sad, it may be a good exercise to look into the mirror, smile and say: "Whatever I feel like, I *know* that my Redeemer lives!" But to smile in order to project a joyful image when you are sick with heartache is to be phoney. You will say, "But I ought not be sick at heart." Perhaps not. But if it is wrong to be worried, it is even more wrong to try to fool people about your worry. Two sins don't add up to obedience. It would be far better to say to a non-Christian, "I know that as a Christian I should have lots of joy, but right now I don't." Witnessing and projecting an image are not the same thing.

So when you witness, do not pretend to be something you are not or to know things you don't know. *Christ may want people to discover you are weak and foolish.* He wants them to be impressed by what *he* can do in the life of a weak and foolish human being. "We have this treasure," Paul stated, "in earthen vessels, to show that the transcendent power belongs to God and not to us" (2 Cor. 4:7).

I cannot emphasize too much that our job as witnesses is not to project a good image. I failed utterly to appreciate this when I was a younger Christian.

Put off by the ludicrous witness strategies of my fellow

Christians, I decided to be more discreet. The result was that I became simply a nice guy. ("He's a little bit religious, but sensible, very sensible. You can't help but like him.") I had my sensors probing for possible areas of embarrassment and did a superb job of deflecting serious conversation, four moves in advance. But I lacked the firmness of a good diplomat. I was too busy avoiding trouble. I was much more concerned with what people thought of me rather than what they thought of Christ.

My chameleon-like skill consisted in adopting the postures and attitudes of people around me. In any verbal traffic between two human beings certain matters are *assumed* to be true. If you make a flippant comment about someone, for instance, you assume that the person you are speaking to sees life the same way you do. He may not; though chances are he will pretend he does, in which case the two of you are not communicating at all. You are both addressing the imaginary person you think the other one is.

In my case I would be busy adopting the mindsets and the viewpoints of the people all round me. I could laugh at their jokes without asking myself whether I really thought them funny; I could cap a cynical comment with an even more cynical one, without pausing to discover whether my own attitude was cynical or not. I was on the way to becoming a nonperson, a mere echo of other people's egos —or worse still what I *thought* were their egos.

On Being Real

Let me review the principles I have been formulating. The essence of witnessing consists of an open declaration of truth you have experienced. A phoney witness is a poor witness; an honest open attitude is the beginning of real witness. *We find it difficult to witness because we have not learned how to be open.* This is why we feel more comfortable when we are offered easily followed techniques for witness.

I came across a book describing such techniques once. Photographs illustrated the instructions. ("Step 3b: Place your left hand on Bill's right shoulder as in illustration #4. Look him in the eye. Your manner should be confident but gentle. If he avoids eye contact say, 'Bill, look at me.' When you have good eye contact say, 'Bill, I wonder if you'll let me tell you how much Jesus means to me....' ")

I shall never forget the morning I decided as far as possible to be simple and honest in my relationship with others. I made my decision with no thought of the revolution it would effect in my witness. Yet within an hour I was in serious conversation about Christ. And within 24 hours I had seen a man converted. I had made no conscious effort to witness or to "win a soul." Both were direct consequences of my attempt to be real.

But "being real" is hard to practice every minute of every hour. It consists of being free to express your true feelings. I say "being free" to express them to remind you that self-expression is not a *summum bonum* in life. (The perfect man is not the one who always lets us know exactly how he feels. Such a man is an insensitive boor.)

To be real does not mean you must steal when you feel covetous or murder when you feel enraged. It means being free to express ourselves when it is appropriate to do so. But we are unable to be our real selves because we are afraid. Fear seals our lips when we ought to speak, creases our faces with smiles when we are annoyed, makes us say yes when we mean no. To be real is to be free from the fears that enslave us.

Christ wants to give you that kind of freedom. God has accepted all that is behind your mask. It matters little what others think about the real you provided you can be sure of God's love. But old habits are hard to break and if you are like me, you'll have to work on being real. It demands faith and boldness—the qualities needed to be a witness.

Why do you laugh at a dirty joke? Is it because it's funny? (Some sexual jokes are.) Or is it because you don't want people to think you're a wet blanket? Perhaps you don't want to embarrass the person who's telling it? Circumstances vary. No response may be necessary. If you don't think the joke is funny, don't put on a phoney laugh. If some response is demanded, try, "Look, I don't want to embarrass you. I think sex is great. But it's kind of important to me. Maybe too important to joke about lightly." Your rejoinder, if it is an honest one, may pave the way to a conversation with a more serious tone.

A conversation of any kind, joking, serious, disgruntled or whatever, turns inevitably into witness if you have the courage to be yourself simply because Christ is important to you. You don't have to look for "openings." Just be you.

To be real means *to be real about something and to be loyal to someone*. You are to be loyal to Jesus Christ who has become the supreme reality in your life. You are not to deny him any more than you are to do an elaborate cover-up job on your own weaknesses.

For the Christian the essence of honesty lies in being faithful not only to the truth but to the Truth. It means not denying Christ. It means that your whole life must now pivot around the commitment that he has made to you and you to him. Your every action, every thought, every word are true or false according to how they measure up to that central commitment.

How Real Was Peter?

One of the most poignant stories in the Gospels concerns Peter's stormy denial of Christ and of his subsequent restoration on the beach one early morning. Shortly before Jesus was arrested he warned his disciples of his approaching passion and predicted that Peter would deny him before dawn. Peter protested his loyalty vehemently (Lk. 22:

31-34). In a futile gesture to back up his protests, he perpetrated the one violent act to characterize Christ's arrest. He slashed an ear off the head of a member of the arresting party (Jn. 18:10-11).

As Jesus majestically took charge of his own arrest, encouraging the frightened soldiers to take him, the disciples took to their heels. Peter and John, however, hung back and followed the arresting party. Because of John's connections in the household of the high priest, both were later admitted to the courtyard, an area crowded with the high priest's servants, a number of soldiers and officers.

Peter may well have been frightened and with good reason. The whole business of following Jesus had suddenly taken a dramatic and sinister turn. The majesty of the palace, the security and jocular ease of the people in the courtyard would make him feel the insecurity of his own position more keenly.

In the night hours that followed he denied his master on three occasions (Jn. 18:15-27; Lk. 22:54-62). He may have excused his denials as a matter of his survival and a tactic of war. He had already protested his loyalty to Jesus too strongly. Doubtless he was struggling to maintain to himself how loyal he really was. After all, was he not in the courtyard of his Master's enemies? Yet at the third denial, the crowing of a cock and a simultaneous glance from Jesus shattered his silly delusion. He suddenly saw himself for the sentimental, weak, impetuous fool that he really was. Overwhelmed with shame he left the courtyard and wept bitterly.

It is impossible to know at exactly what point Peter had begun to deny Christ. Certainly in his attitude and by his actions he must have been denying him long before he did so verbally. The denial that sprang to his lips at the first accusation must already have been present in his demeanor. He was playing a part, a part in which he fooled himself and tried to fool people around him. The need to be liked remained in his character for as long as history records. And it is our own need to be liked that causes us by a thousand subtle gestures to deny Christ today. Much of my own flippancy was precisely that sort of denial. It was a cover up for my embarrassing relationship to Jesus Christ.

Peter loved Christ and so did I. Like a man torn between his mistress and his wife, Peter loved two things at the same time, the admiration of other people and the presence of his master. It was an uncomfortable situation to be in. Neither mistresses nor wives are willing to give in to one another. As a jealous spouse Christ wants and claims absolute loyalty from his followers. And that means that by every action, every thought, every word you must be loyal to him and not conceal your loyalty.

So at the heart of witness lies integrity in a personal relationship. If you would be a faithful witness, turn your thoughts constantly to God. Let it become your habit in every encounter with other people and as you turn to every activity to say, "Lord, I am nothing but your blood-bought servant. Help me to behave as such now."

Be courteous. Don't make it your aim to impress others by the brilliance of your repartee. Don't try to be the center of attention or the monopolizer of the conversation. Aim rather at putting others at their ease. Don't pretend to know things you don't know. If you argue, try to understand what the other person is saying. You should not try to win a verbal fencing match so much as to understand and be understood.

If you are real, your actions and words will match. You will find yourself glad to perform acts of courtesy and consideration for a roommate, for family members. You will be less inclined to borrow and more prompt to return or to lend to others. You will be more punctual at handing in assignments. You will be less of a grouch. You will not suddenly become perfect. But when you behave badly, you will recognize that an apology is owed and make the apology. Where you don't find yourself behaving generously, God will show you and you will be grieved. You will be willing to own up to your weakness to God, to other Christians and to non-Christians. And if someone compliments you on your character, you will not say: "Aw shucks, it's nothing," but "Thanks. I haven't always been that way though. I used to be quite different."

Hostile Reactions

There have been times in history when a tyrant would lop off the heads of any messengers who brought him bad tidings. Peter, if we may get back to him for a moment, was facing more than ridicule. He was in danger of his life. People around you are not likely to be quite so hostile when you talk about Christ, yet not all will respond positively. The Greek word translated "witness" in the New Testament is the word from which we derive our English word martyr. Such was the persecution early Christians encountered that witnessing and martyrdom become two sides of the same coin. It is possible that during our own lifetime in the West the same may happen again.

People's reactions to learning of Christ have ranged from murderous paranoid hatred to eager glad acceptance. Sometimes it has provoked nothing more than mild amusement or interested curiosity.

You must recognize beforehand that people will react and sometimes react strongly. If you are unprepared, you may feel that *you* are to blame for what has happened, whereas it may have nothing to do with you at all.

I remember a violent reaction to a remark I made to a psychiatrist who was supervising part of my residency training. He was treating a homosexual patient by teaching him in easy stages how to date and how to make love to girls—in fact how to seduce them. I commented that my religious convictions would make it difficult for me to use the same method. His face flushed with anger and he spat contempt at me.

Had that incident taken place a few years previously, I would have been filled with anxiety and guilt, wondering where I had gone wrong. As it was I merely made a mental note that my supervisor had hang-ups in the areas of religion and sex. Though I forbore to press the point, dismissing it with a shrug of my shoulders, I continued to be completely open with him about the Christian convictions I had.

Remember: People will react to you. A favorable reaction does not mean you are witnessing skillfully any more than a hostile reaction means that you have blown it. By all means be self-critical and check to see whether you have not been tactless, rude, critical, discourteous or opinionated. However, the reaction may tell you something not about yourself but about the person to whom you are bearing witness.

A hostile reaction is to be welcomed. It may be a sign that you have prodded a sore spot. No one could have displayed a more diabolical ferocity against Christian witness than Saul of Tarsus; yet his very fury was a measure of his own desperate struggle with his conscience. "It is hard for you to kick against the goad" was Christ's apt comment (see Acts 9:5).

If you *know* that strong reactions are to be welcomed, you will be less likely to fall into the trap of getting angry yourself or of becoming defensive or argumentative. The Holy Spirit will give you both compassion and perceptiveness for those who so react.

A strong reaction may take the form of criticism against you or Christians generally. Words like "hypocrisy," "cant," "unscientific" and "escapism" may bombard you. My reaction as a psychiatrist is usually one of, "You seem to feel pretty strongly about this. Why?" I don't suggest you copy me, but I do urge you not to fall into the trap of defending the actions and attitudes of your fellow Christians or yourself.

It must, of course, be obvious to you that in telling what Christ has done for you, you are not being called on to justify the Crusades, or 20th-century Christian materialism any more than you can justify the failure and sin of many Christian groups. A more appropriate response in such situations might follow the lines of, "Yes. A good many evil things have been done in the name of Christianity. But are the Crusades really what keep you from believing that Christ is alive?"

The Need to Know More

This brings me to the point I have been dodging all along. Since the beginning of the chapter I have studiously avoided giving you a set speech to use in your witness. Many of us would feel more secure if we could memorize a set speech and trot it out like the salesman. At least one Christian organization encourages its members to write out the story of their conversion, memorize it and then use it whenever they have an opportunity.

I have already objected to such a procedure on moral grounds. I would add the criticism that no two personal encounters are the same and that to repeat the same words in every encounter involves the risk of being insensitive to the real needs of the person I am talking to.

In part then I have been saying: Tell it like it is by responding honestly and naturally to the person you are with. Be loyal to Christ moment by moment and the words will look after themselves.

However, I must add a caveat. Honesty will at times compel you to admit your ignorance of certain aspects of your faith. There is no reason to be ashamed of not knowing everything; but neither is there any good reason to remain ignorant about your faith. Make it your lifelong task to have an ever more profound grasp of the basis of your faith. Become an expert in it. Don't be satisfied with memorizing a few proof texts (however valuable these may be), but get a grasp of "the whole counsel of God," in order that you may become able to give a clear account of why you believe what you believe.

Begin today. Make use of your personal time of quiet as well as group Bible study. Honesty and ignorance don't have to be married. Your knowledge must not be allowed to make you conceited or to play one-upmanship with people you talk to. But you must seek earnestly to "always be prepared to make a defense to anyone who calls you to account for the hope that is in you, yet do it with gentleness and reverence" (1 Pet. 3:15). We are instructed "in malice ... be children, but in understanding be men" (1 Cor. 14: 20, KJV).

Summary

You are a witness whether you want to be one or not. Either you are a good witness or a poor one.

A good witness tells the truth about what he has personally discovered. In doing so he acts like a signpost pointing others to Christ.

Witnessing techniques are to be used with caution. They are never a substitute for personal honesty or for the power of the Holy Spirit.

The task of a witness is not to convert people nor to "clinch a deal" but to supply them with the data by means of which the Holy Spirit brings conviction to them.

To supply them with adequate data you will need to add to your personal experience a comprehensive grasp of why you believe what you believe.

A Passage to Study

Read John 4:1-30, 39-42.

1. Some people say Jesus sat on the well in order to get a chance of talking to the woman. What evidence is there in the passage to support or to undermine this hypothesis?

2. At the sixth hour (verse 6) the sun is high. It has been suggested that Jesus' request for water was an opening evangelistic gambit. The evidence is less conclusive here but do you think his request arose from thirst or as a stratagem? Give your reasons.

3. Verses 9, 19-20. How did Jesus respond to the woman's argument?

4. Verses 29-30, 41-42. Notice and comment on the relationship in the making of converts between: (a) the woman's words of testimony and (b) the word of Christ. How can the lesson apply to your own witness?

5

His Infernal Majesty

I stated in chapter one that your relationship with the Evil One has changed.

You may not have realized you had a relationship with him at all (unless you were fooling around with the occult). Yet aware of it or no, his spirit was at work in your body (Eph. 2:2). Unknown to you, his deceptions obscured your thinking while his music inflamed your senses and influenced your will. He thought of himself as your master; but like credit rating agencies he made himself as unobtrusive as possible. His greatest skill lay in giving you the feeling that you were your own master.

C. S. Lewis's remark, that humanity falls into two equal and opposite errors concerning the devil, is now more famous than the book (*The Screwtape Letters*) in which it is found. The errors, according to Lewis, consist either in taking the devil altogether too seriously or in not taking him seriously enough. The devil welcomes a Hume or a Faust with equal zest. He is equally delighted by an atheist, a liberal theologian or a witch. And, it may be added, he feels as happy with a Christian whose mind is preoccupied with demons all day long as he is with one who never gives them a thought.

But he is living and virulent. His supreme object is to hurt Christ and Christ's cause. You personally are of no interest to him. It is only as you relate to Christ that you assume significance in his eyes. Before you became a Christian he was mainly interested in blinding you to the truth of Christ or perhaps in seducing you further into his terrain. But this was not because of your personal importance. He only used you to get back at God. Similarly, now that you are a Christian his interest in you has nothing to do with you as an individual so much as with your potential for Christ's cause. Do not flatter yourself. To God you are very important. But to Satan you are nothing more than a potentially useful microbe.

But microbe or no he can hurt you. He and his hellions will damage you along one or more of four lines: They will *tempt,* they will *accuse,* they will *deceive* and they will *devour.*

Temptation without Dismay

You will be tempted. The kinds of temptation may change: Candies for kids, sensuality for the young, riches for the middle aged and power for the aging. The Evil One can ring the changes with greater skill than any advertising agency. He knows the Achilles' heel (if I may mix my metaphor) of every microbe.

You will be tempted continuously. You will be tempted ferociously at times of crisis. Jesus himself was tempted "in all points as we are" (that is, to commit adultery, to steal, to lie, to kill and on and on) *"yet without sin."*

Therefore temptation itself need not dismay you. It was your Savior's lot and it will be yours. As long as you live you will be tempted. But if temptation is no cause for dismay, it is likewise no excuse for sin. Nowhere in Scripture are we justified by praying, "Lord it's true I sinned, but you see the devil tempted me." This was the first prayer of confession in the Garden of Eden ("The serpent tricked me and I ate" Gen. 3:13, NEB), and it didn't wash with God. James is contemptuous of any attempt by a Christian to slough off his responsibility for sin. "Each person is tempted when he is lured and enticed *by his own desire.* Then desire when it has conceived gives birth to sin" (Jas. 1:14-15).

There is no inconsistency between James' view that temptation is a man's inner lusts (inordinate internal desires) and the view that he is lured by satanic appeal.

Have you ever fooled around with a piano? Open the top. Press the loud pedal. Then sing a note into the piano as loudly as you can. Stop and listen. You will hear at least one cord vibrating in response to the note you sang. You sing—and a string in the piano picks up your voice and plays it back.

Here, then, is a picture of temptation. Satan calls and you vibrate. The vibration is the "lust" James speaks of. Your desire is to go on responding to his call. If pianos have feeling, I imagine they are "turned on" when the cord vibrates. There is nothing bad about vibrating. The cord was made to vibrate and to vibrate powerfully. But it was meant to vibrate in response to a hammer—not in response to a voice.

The appropriate response, then, is not to vibrate rapturously to the voice of the devil but to release the loud pedal and close the top of the piano. As Luther put it quaintly, you cannot stop birds flying about your head, but you can prevent them from building a nest in your hair.

In more concrete terms, whether vibration consists of sexual arousal, angry feelings, a desire to possess something beautiful or whatever, *the vibration itself is not evil.* Sexual arousal has its place. The question is under what circumstances? Or again, is *this* the appropriate object and *this* the appropriate occasion? If not, slam down the lid of the piano and get your big foot off the loud pedal!

While there exists an infinite variety of notes the devil can whistle, his temptations fall under three broad groupings: the lust of the flesh, the lust of the eye and the pride of life.

Put in modern terms, these groupings refer to a basic problem in Christian living. A *desire* may be your servant; a *lust* is your master. The lust of the flesh means to be dominated by your physical appetites: hunger, thirst, the need for sleep, the desire for sex or for physical exercise. Obviously physical appetites are wholesome. Generally they are meant to be satisfied. But we live in an age when eating, drinking and "the great sexual experience" are presented to us as goals in themselves. People bow down and worship them. They live to eat (or to copulate), instead of accepting food and sex with gratitude and in their proper place.

The lust of the eye means to have your life governed by a love of beautiful things whether you conceive of beauty in terms of a Mazeratti, a black tulip or an original Picasso. There is nothing wrong with liking or wanting beautiful things. God is a God of beauty. But the passion to possess and hoard beauty is a lust that can destroy Christian living.

I once went to dinner with a Chinese businessman who was in his early sixties. His house was breathtakingly beautiful. A tree whose leaves were semiprecious stones dominated the foyer. In the dining room we ate with gold utensils. Exquisite taste subdued what otherwise might have seemed like ostentation. My host revealed a profound knowledge of biblical doctrine and professed to be a Christian. His ambition was to have enough money to preach the gospel "without being a burden to anyone." His spiritual activity at the time was nil and his heart was as dry as dust.

The pride of life has mainly to do with ambition. Again, ambition is good. God implants in our beings the desire to excel. But excellence too can become a tyrant, dominating our whole view of life. I may excuse excessive ambition as wanting to excel "for Christ" when the real inner need is to excel to prove something of myself. You must do serious thinking about your ambitions and ask yourself, "Is ambition my master or my servant?"

The three lusts—of the flesh, of the eye and of ambition —correspond to three psychological responses Eve gave to the primal satanic temptation. "The woman saw that the tree was good for food (the lust of the flesh), and that it was a delight to the eyes (the lust of the eye), that the tree was to be desired to make one wise (the pride of life)" (Gen. 3:6).

They also call to mind Satan's three-pronged attacks on our Savior: " 'Command this stone to become bread' (the lust of the flesh). . . . 'Throw yourself down' (the pride of life). . . . The devil took him up, and showed him all the kingdoms of the world in a moment of time. . . . 'It shall all be yours' (the lust of the eye and the pride of life)" (Lk. 4: 1-15).

Yet we should not concern ourselves with the form of temptation but with how to resist it. Let me be very simple. Satan tempts *from behind*. "Look," he whispers, "Isn't it beautiful? Just think what you could do . . . what people would say . . . how you would be admired . . . how much power you would have . . . look, *look*, LOOK!" The Bible gives us two complementary counsels about temptation, one on temptation itself and the other on the tempter. Concerning temptation we are simply told: Flee temptation. Concerning the tempter the word is: Resist the devil, *and he will flee from you.*

Think how these two counsels work together. Did you ever run away from something and face it at the same time? How could you?

Never face temptation. Flee from it. And in fleeing, *turn* your back on it. And in turning, whom will you face? Who has been standing behind you and whispering vivid word-pictures in your ear? Turn and face him. Resist him. And his Satanic Majesty will withdraw.

But how do you resist?

Well, turning is three-quarters of the battle. Later we will discuss what Paul calls "the whole armor of God." For the present let me confine myself to one piece of that armor which he calls "the sword of the Spirit ... the Word of God."

Many commentators have pointed out that when Jesus was tempted in the wilderness he responded to each satanic suggestion with the words, "it is written ... it is written.... it is written." Each time that Jesus employed the sword of the Spirit, he slashed the tempter.

Many Christians have testified to the astonishing effect particular Scriptures have in their ability to cope with temptation. The Bible is called the sword of the Spirit for three reasons: The Spirit inspired it; the Spirit will place it in your hands and teach you skill in using it; the Spirit will make it cut deep. Therefore get to know Scripture. And as you turn your back on temptation and face your Tempter, reach out your hand for the sword which the Spirit will place in your grasp. Then plunge it deep into the Tempter and hear him howl in pain as he flees back to hell from before a "microbe with an Achilles' heel."

Accusation of the Brethren

Oh, how he loves to accuse you! "Now the salvation and the power and the kingdom of our God and the authority of his Christ have come, for the accuser of our brethren has been thrown down, who accuses them day and night before our God" (Rev. 12:10).

He accuses. Accuses whom? He accuses the brethren; that is to say all Christians. He accuses *you*. To this day he tries to ape the counsel for the crown.

Where does he accuse? He accuses you "before our God." When you kneel to pray his accusations will echo through the vault of your skull. When you seek to bear witness to Jesus, he will scream to God of your vile unworthiness; and if ever you try to preach in public—watch out! He will rant and rave before God in your hearing about the foulness of the lips that attempt to preach God's Word.

When does he accuse? He accuses day and night. As you wake for a moment in the night he will still be accusing. In your dreams he will accuse. You will drink your morning coffee with a tablespoonful of denunciation and do your day's work against a background of accusation muzak.

So naturally you will feel guilty. Feelings of guilt will take the sparkle out of your eye and the snap out of your step. They will dull the edge of your witness, take the heart out of Christian service and make any public testimony as stale as moldy fish. And this is precisely what Satan has in mind. Accusation is his secret weapon, supremely effective in taking the zap out of the Christian army's attack. How could guilt-ridden soldiers possibly assail the gates of hell?

"But hold on," you say. "Does guilt not arise from sin, and should sin not always be confessed?" To the second part of your question: Yes. Sin should always be confessed and where necessary, restitution should be made. There will always be sin to confess (1 Jn. 1:8-9). But to the first part of your question: No. Guilt does not always imply sin.

Psychoanalysts speak of neurotic guilt, guilt feelings which arise because of our early experiences. In doing so they are trying to explain why we feel guilty. But their theories raise serious questions: Do feelings of guilt necessarily mean I have sinned? Is *felt* guilt *true* guilt? Can consciences (or superego) always be trusted? These issues are of paramount importance. Satan has no power to paralyze the hosts of heaven with true guilt (Christ's death is sufficient to take care of that). False guilt is the weapon he uses most. And false guilt means *feeling guilty when I have no reason to*. It is Accuser-induced guilt. The late Dr. Donald Grey Barnhouse frequently gave a brilliant illustration of the limitations of conscience. Conscience, he used to tell us, is like a sundial (one of those flat-topped curios you find in Old English gardens, bearing Roman numerals and a shadow pointing to the time).

A sundial only works when there is light. It does not work at midnight in a fog. Moreover it requires light from the proper source. The moon makes it point to the wrong time. Take a flashlight with you and walk around a sundial at 3:00 A.M. It will tell you whatever time you want. Conscience, likewise, functions only when it has the light of God's Word illuminated by God's Spirit, shining on it.

When psychoanalysts raise the question of false (neurotic) guilt then, they are raising a perfectly biblical point. We may disagree with them as to the *content* of false guilt (that is to say about what should make you feel guilty and what shouldn't), but about the existence of the phenomenon they are right on the ball.

John Bunyan in his exciting book *The Holy War* describes the capture of the town of Mansoul by Apollyon's forces. A principal citizen of Mansoul was Mr. Conscience, the town crier. It was the duty of Mr. Conscience to warn Mansoul of danger and to announce celebrations and glad tidings.

Following the city's capture by Prince Apollyon, the town crier became insane. Peril might loom over the city yet Mr. Conscience would remain wrapped in moody silence in his watchtower. Yet in the night while all men slept he would shriek his crazy warning of non-existent ills or sing insanely of joys that were not to be.

All this was Bunyan's graphic way of telling us that the conscience of fallen man has gone awry. It can live in comfort with some sin yet be unbelievably sensitive about things that are not sin at all. Nor are matters automatically rectified when a man becomes a Christian. Certainly his conscience is quickened, but wrong training from the past still interferes with its proper functioning.

How then may I know what is right from what is wrong? How may I rid myself of the appalling burden of *false* guilt? How may I know the difference between the accusations of Satan and the conviction of the Holy Spirit?

I suppose there is a long-range answer and a short-range answer in the matter of conscience and its proper functioning. The long-range answer has to do with Scripture. Day by day, week by week, year by year my conscience must be reinstructed, reoriented by a progressive knowledge of God's Word. Just as the compass in a sailing boat must be "swung," that is, rechecked and modified while the boat is made to face in every direction, so over the years a Christian's conscience becomes ever more finely and accurately tuned as practical experience in Scripture is gained under the Spirit's tutelage. All the while the Christian's behavior must be modified by what he learns from Scripture. He must sail according to the corrected compass.

Yet the short-range answer is every bit as important and will remain so to the end of your days. The Spirit convicts; the Enemy accuses. How may I know which voice is which?

Think of it logically for a moment.

What is the Enemy trying to *do* when he accuses? And the Spirit when he convicts? Clearly the Enemy seeks to *destroy* your fellowship with God. The Spirit, on the other hand, is attempting to *restore* your fellowship with God. (And here it may be worthwhile to note that the Accuser often tells the truth. The sins and failures he accuses me of are not always false. Sometimes they correspond to reality.)

Now if the Spirit is attempting to *restore* your fellowship with God, it follows that when sin is confessed, conviction will melt away and the blossom of fellowship burst out with new fragrance. It also follows that if Satan is bent on *destroying* your fellowship with God and if your sense of sin results from satanic accusation, then no such fragrance will be experienced. It will seem to you rather that your confession has somehow been inadequate, that you need to be more thoroughgoing in your analysis of your sin, more rigorous in your restitution. Yet to your dismay the confession is never thoroughgoing enough. "What was your *real* motive in that 'good' deed?" a voice will ask. "Are you *sure* you have left nothing out? Can't you *sense* that you're only skimming the surface? Don't you see how deceit permeates your heart like a vile poison?" In horror you will recoil at the ever broadening vision of your own evil. First greyness, then blackness will envelop you as a cloud; and you will sit in huddled, shivering misery wrapped in the center of your own cold shadow. The Accuser will have achieved his objective.

Now the only place in Scripture where the devil is actually *named* the Accuser is in the twelfth chapter of the book of Revelation. In the same chapter, in the very next sentence, we read that the brethren "conquered him (as the Accuser) by the blood of the Lamb."

Much nonsense has been talked and much tomfoolery acted out around the sacred words "the blood of Jesus."

Let it be understood that the words have no magic in them. They do not constitute a spell. They should never be used as an incantation. It may be true that the response to the words "the blood of Jesus" can indeed be dramatic. Hobgoblins and foul fiends are jumpy creatures.

But in reference to the Accuser their meaning is precise. Blood in Scripture symbolizes death, *always* death and usually violent or sacrificial death. ("His blood be upon us and upon our children." "The avenger of blood," and so forth.) Even where it seems to speak of life, it speaks of it only as life poured out in death. So when John says that the brethren overcame the Accuser by the blood of the Lamb, he is really telling us that they overcame his accusations by the death of Christ.

The second thing you must understand about blood is that it was given to *cleanse our consciences*. In hymnology we sing about our hearts being washed in the blood of Jesus. The tunes may be musical but the theology grates. "For, if the sprinkling of defiled persons with the blood of goats and bulls . . . sanctifies," writes the author of the Hebrew epistle, "how much more shall the blood of Christ . . . purify your conscience from dead works to serve the living God" (Heb. 9:13-14).

Try to understand the verse. All along we have been considering the satanic strategy of destroying your fellowship with God by creating a guilty conscience in you. God's answer to your guilty conscience is the death of his Son. *Your* answer to a guilty conscience is usually something you *do*, like confessing harder, praying more, reading your Bible, paying more than your tithe in the offering and so on. These actions are what the writer to the Hebrews calls "dead works," the very things your conscience needs to be cleansed from and the very things that eventually get you wrapped up in the black shadow of your own guilt.

Consider another verse in the Hebrew letter. "Let us draw near with a true heart in full assurance of faith, with our hearts sprinkled clean from an evil conscience and our bodies washed with pure water" (Heb. 10:22). There you have it. Water for the body but blood for the conscience. And notice the context.

Do you know how to go *boldly* into the presence of God the Holy One? Or do you, as I hinted in chapter one, find yourself creeping into his presence, head down and shoulders slumped? The difference between the one approach and the other has to do with your conscience. A man with a clean conscience runs into God's presence, arms widely spread, like a child leaping into the embrace of his father. Is that how you come?

Do you not understand? The Father does not welcome you because you have been trying hard, because you have made a thoroughgoing confession or because you have been making spiritual strides recently. He does not welcome you because you have something you can be proud about. He welcomes you because *his Son died for you.* His breast has always yearned for you and his arms yearned to enfold you. Christ's death has now made it possible for the Father to do what he wanted to do all along. So come boldly—sprinkled by blood. Let him enfold you to the warmth of his bosom while his hot tears wash over your body.

Hot tears? Does the expression sound irreverent or sentimental? I have no words that do justice to the love that led to the death of God's Son. The universe ought to have stopped in its tracks, and I, for one, am sorry it didn't. No more heinous crime was ever committed against God nor greater act of love consummated on behalf of the criminal. Are you blasphemous enough to suppose that your dead works, your feeble efforts can add to the finished work of a dying Savior? "It is finished!" he cried. Completed. Done. Forever ended. He crashed through the gates of hell, set prisoners free, abolished death and burst in new life from the tomb. All to set you free from sin and open the way for you to run into the loving arms of God.

Now do you understand how "the brethren" overcame the Accuser by the blood of the Lamb? *They refused to let his accusations impede their access to God.* A simple confession was enough. They faced the Accuser boldly saying, "We already know the worst you could ever tell us and so does God. What is more the blood of Jesus is enough."

Well may the Accuser roar
Of ills that I have done:

I know them all, and thousands more:
Jehovah knoweth none![2]
Therefore when you find the grey cloud descending, whether it be as you pray, as you work, as you testify or whatever, when you find the ring of assurance going from your words because of a vague sense of guilt, look up to God and say, "Thank you my Father for the blood of your Son. Thank you even now that you accept me gladly, lovingly in spite of all I am and have done—because of his death. Father and God, I come."

Say it to him now. Say it sitting, kneeling or standing. Do not wait a moment. Your Heavenly Father is waiting for you. He misses you. He bids you come. Now. Sprinkled by blood.

Deception Overcome
But the brethren also overcame Satan by the word of their testimony. Look at Revelation 12 and perhaps you will see why. He is described there in three roles. He is, as we have already seen, the Accuser. He is also "that ancient serpent ... the deceiver of the whole world." And he is described as a dragon devouring and making war (referred to elsewhere as the "roaring lion").

Christians overcome Satan, the deceiving serpent, by the "word of their testimony." In doing so they launch their warfare into enemy-held territory. Freed from a sense of guilt and therefore ready to do battle with a single mind, they launch an attack on the satanic darkness with penetrating rays of light.

"The deceiver of the whole world." He began by deceiving Eve.

"Did God really say that? Well now, he was hardly speaking the truth. The fact of the matter is. . . ."

And just as did Eve, so millions of her descendants have been falling for the ploy ever since. Paul describes Satan as "the God of this world [who] hath blinded the minds of them that believe not, lest the light of knowledge...." Blinded minds. Deceived hearts.

Deceived through TV ads and university educations. Use pink toilet paper and you'll be happy. Buy a shiny car and a pretty lady will get in it. Invest in real estate and insurance and you'll be safe. Smell nice and bed nice. Sex makes you fulfilled. Get good grades and corporations will love you. Money isn't everything, *but*....

Talk sociological gobbledygook and people will bow before your wisdom. Let's all learn to accept death without the need of superstitious fantasies of what lies beyond. Science says there is no God. Science says there *is* a God. Science says Genesis is true, so it must be. It's amazing what science will prove. Let us therefore bow down to the latest Hypothesis. Let us kneel before our Transactional Analyst.

Does it all sound too ridiculous to credit? Know then that Satan the deceiver understands his business well. Anyone who can keep you feverishly hunting for the Perfect Deodorant without letting you realize what an ass you are is supremely competent. And if you think that words alone, my words or anyone else's words, will undeceive the blinded minds of "them that believe not" you are a fool. I can make people smile momentarily at their idiocy by my verbal skill, but they'll go right on hunting for the Perfect Deodorant.

No, it is by "the word of [your] testimony" that you will overcome the deceiver. And that means the Word of God that has been proved true by you in your experience and about which you may legitimately testify. Once you are able to say, "The Bible says . . . and it was such a help to me that it really solved my problem," the gates of hell will not prevail against you. The light of your words will pierce the satanic blindness of people around you, and they will begin to see. And when that happens the dragon will swish his powerful tail and sweep a third of heavenly bodies into blackness. He will rage and gnash his teeth for he will know that his end is nearer. Microbes with Achilles' heels will assume a greater importance to him.

Warfare with the Devourer

"Be strong in the Lord and in the strength of his might" (Eph. 6:10).

What chance does a microbe have against Satan? What chance did Bunyan's Christian have against Apollyon? Of what use will *you* be in a battle with the legions of hell?

Please notice: You will be part of the attacking force. If the passage in Ephesians sounds like advice for *defense*, it is defense against *counterattack*. Once you are committed to giving the word of your testimony you are part of Christ's attacking army. You are invading enemy-held territory.

But being part of Christ's army entitles you to all of heaven's resources. The might of Jehovah is at your disposal. So be strong *in the Lord.*

"Good advice," you may say, "but in concrete terms how may I be strong *in the Lord?*" You may be so by having no confidence in your own ability, by doing what God says and trusting him to back you, by exercising what is called "the obedience of faith," by stepping, at God's command, towards closed glass doors and watching them swing open as you reach them. Your strength lies in what *he* does when *you* obey.

Yet the counterattack will come against you. So you will need armor, for the principalities and powers will send their legions to assail you. "Put on the whole armor of God" so that their counterattack will fail. Armor against what? Armor against wiles. Against cunning and trickery. To be sure the metaphor is mixed, but get your Bible out and open it at Ephesians 6:10-18 as you go on reading this chapter. Let us look at each piece of equipment the passage mentions.

What kind of armor will resist *cunning*? Well, you begin with the belt of *truth* (v. 14). Basic to all your defense must be an accurate perception of the way things really are. ("Hath God said?" "Yes, God *hath* said—and that's good enough for me!") Reality, for our purposes, may be defined as *things the way God sees and reveals them.*

The breastplate of righteousness is a metaphorical alternative for a blood-sprinkled conscience. Your defense against the spear thrust of accusation is, as we have already learned, the solid assurance that the Father accepts you completely because of the death of the Son. To put on the breastplate of righteousness is another way of saying to overcome by the blood of the Lamb.

I am a little uncertain about the military footware Paul recommends (v. 15). Commentaries differ. It sounds as though he is saying you should get a solid footing in your grasp of the Christian gospel. But the "shield of faith" is straightforward enough. Whatever flaming darts—of fear, of dismay, of pain—may be flung at you, catch them with a bold affirmation of your confidence in Christ. He is alive. He is in control. Look up to him and tell him you will trust him come what may, and the flaming darts will sputter and die.

The helmet of salvation has to do with Christian hope (1 Thess. 5:8). It is fashionable nowadays in psychiatry to stress the importance of the "here-and-now." Who cares what happened when I was three years old? What does it matter where I shall be ten years hence? It's *now* that matters.

And so it is. But we must not be too hasty to dump past and future into the garbage can. To the Christian the past matters intensely and the future does too. The here-and-now can only be *understood* in the light of the past and only *faced* in the light of the future. Life without hope is death in the here-and-now.

And Christ gives you hope. Present chaos will not endure. There is cosmic hope of a restitution of all things. Christ will judge and Christ will restore. There is personal hope. You will take part in that same restoration. Don't live *in* the future but work *for* it, and your skull will be well protected.

So stand when the counterattack comes. Stand with all the firmness of a true believer. Pray unceasingly but pray on your feet. And the counterattack, however fierce, will suddenly die away. You will discover that what happened to Christ will happen to you. The enemy will depart and leave you alone for a little while (Lk. 4:13).

At least he will almost always do so. I must not leave you with the false impression that there are no casualties in the battle. Let me remind you of the four roles that Satan has in his opposition to Christ. He is the tempter, the accuser, the deceiver and the devourer. When he neither tempts you nor stops you from bearing witness by incapacitating you with guilt, you will find yourself encountering him as the deceiver of the whole world. And once you start to overcome him by the word of your testimony, he will henceforth assume mainly the roles of the roaring lion and the devouring dragon.

Let me be clear what I am talking about. Satan is not now trying to devour your soul but to kill or maim your body. God usually doesn't let him. But again let me say we are not engaged in play-war but in a real one. Christ himself was crucified battling to conquer death and hell and to rise again.

Paradoxically, it is in his role as the devouring dragon that we see Satan's hopeless weakness. When he kills someone he has reached the nadir of frustration and hopelessness. Christ in his death won his greatest victory.

He hell, in hell, laid low;
Made sin, He sin o'erthrew;

Bow'd to the grave, destroyed it so;
And death, by dying, slew.[3]

When we say that martyr blood is the seed of the church,
we are not whitewashing tragedy with a sentimental cliché
but stating a simple fact. When Ayore Indians bludgeoned
five New Tribes missionaries to death in the Bolivian jungle
in the early 1940s, there arose, even during wartime in the
U.S., a tremendous surge of new missionary interest. The
five were replaced by fifty. There is now a growing Ayore
church.

When a couple of decades later another five independent missionaries were murdered by Auca Indians in Ec-
uador, the same thing happened. Missionary work among
primitive tribal people has not been the same since.

Let me state it in simple terms. Satan cannot hurt you
until your task for Christ is completed. Until that time
comes you are truly immortal. He may roar. He may threat-
en. But he is powerless.

When your earthly task *is* completed (and it may be completed when you are young), it is possible that he may kill
you. But you will achieve by your death as much and more
than by your life. *Satan is powerless to stop the advance of the
gospel through your life.*

Last night I had a long, vivid dream. I'm sure I must have
been thinking of this chapter. My dream was set in Pendleton, a semi-slum area where I was brought up for awhile as
a child. It no longer exists. The air (in my dream) was filled
with terror because virulent hatred and violence reigned in
Pendleton. Ugliness darkened the streets. The people were
afraid. Somehow I knew I had to devote the rest of my life
to their distress.

At the climax of the dream, I saw a man murdered by
being dragged to the prison bars which covered the window
of his bedroom and held by an invisible force, while his
face and the front of his body were torn from him.

I was shocked and sickened by so dreadful an end to a man's life and appalled that he was so quickly beyond help. I was moved to comfort terrified people around me. But the bloody, mangled remains still sticking against the cagelike bars of the man's bedroom window were clearly a warning to me. It was a message to me to leave Pendleton.

Yet in that moment I knew that my enemies had lost. Evil powers could not make me leave Pendleton and *that* was what they really wanted to achieve by their threat. It wasn't my death that they wanted but to make me turn back. And when the threat of death no longer affected me, there was nothing more that they could do. They were defeated. I exulted in the knowledge of my triumph.

Running through this chapter as a leitmotif has been the motto of CICCU, the Cambridge Inter-Collegiate Christian Union in Britain. It is the verse I quoted earlier: Revelation 12:11. Let me summarize what I have been saying.

It seems to me (and the idea is not an original one) that in this verse "the brethren" overcame Satan in three ways. They overcame him as the Accuser by the blood of the Lamb. They overcame him as the deceiving serpent by the word of their testimony. And they overcame him as the devouring dragon because they loved not their lives unto the death.

Such people are invincible. Nothing can stop them, and nothing ever will.

And tho this world, with devils filled,
Should threaten to undo us;
We will not fear, for God hath willed
His truth to triumph through us:...
Let goods and kindred go,
This mortal life also;
The body they may kill:

God's truth abideth still,
His Kingdom is forever.[4]

A Passage to Study
Read Ephesians 6:10-20.

1. The passage begins with the word "Finally." Skim through the section from 4:25—6:9 to get the general drift of the context of the passage.

2. Why would Paul bother to say that we are not contending with flesh and blood (v. 12)? What bearing does the statement have on our relations with: (a) non-Christians, (b) fellow Christians, (c) members of our family?

3. What general area of the body is offered no protection by any of the armor mentioned—even by a shield? Is it possible to draw inferences from this absence of protection?

4. Of how much importance is prayer in the battle? How able are you personally to carry out verse 18?

6

Faith

Faith is at the core of practical Christianity.
Your Christian life began when you began to believe. It
has grown and will grow as faith widens the channel along
which grace flows to you. No aspect of your Christian life is
of greater importance.

Yet few aspects of Christian living cause more confusion.
"Lord, increase our faith," the disciples pleaded, only to be
told that faith the size of a grain of mustard seed was all that
was required for the most momentous tasks (Mt. 17:20).
Yet if so little was needed, why was their experience so
poor?

Clearly, before we can answer questions of this nature,
we need to understand what faith is.

Man's Response to God's Initiative
Faith is man's response to God's initiative. Your first faith
was the positive response you made to the Holy Spirit when
he brought truth about Christ home to your heart. As God's
light dawned on you, you decided to bow your will to Christ
and to entrust your destiny to him. You could have re-

sponded negatively. The choice was yours. But the process, which was to lead either to rejection or acceptance, began with God.

When the angel appeared to the Virgin Mary to announce her awesome responsibility, she responded with a humble "Let it be the way God has said" (Lk. 1:38). Very few Protestant writers have commented on how much faith Mary had at this point. Yet two things are clear: First, her faith was her response to the Word of God coming to her; and second, through her faith God invaded history.

To realize that faith is your response to something God does or says, will take pressure off you and enable you to adopt a more constructive attitude to it. Do not look inside yourself and ask, "How much faith do I have?" Look to God and ask, "What is he saying to me? What would he have me do?" When Jesus praised the great faith of different men and women in the Gospels, he was not praising a mystical inner state. He was usually commenting on a concrete action by which someone responded to him. It might have been the action of the Roman centurion who sent his servants to Christ asking only that Christ speak the word of power or the pathetic struggle of a feeble woman to touch his robe. Whatever it was, it was the person's response, usually in overt action, to God's call.

Once you understand this you will also begin to see why the amount of faith you have is a less crucial issue than you might have thought. The saying of Jesus about the grain of mustard seed begins to make sense.

How much faith does it take for a non-swimmer to push off the side? Only enough to transfer the support of his body for a fraction of a second from the side of the pool to the water.

How much faith did Martha need to get Lazarus back from the dead? Precious little (Jn. 11:38-40). If we are to go by mystical inner states, every evidence points to Martha having no faith at all. No, what she needed (and what she had) was *enough faith to give orders for the tombstone to be moved,* in spite of the doubts she felt. And Lazarus was raised from the dead.

What about Lazarus himself? Here, I confess, we are dealing with speculation for none of us have experienced death, and Lazarus left no records. But in fantasy I hear the words "Lazarus, come forth" cut through the silence of Lazarus' tomb. What was Lazarus aware of at that point? It was as though the Word of God pulled him upright from the tomb, bewildered and blinking into the sunlight. Or did you just stumble forward when you heard the voice of the Savior?

Actions in most of us involve decision. I see the elevator door open, and I decide to get in. I know that last time when I punched button 15 I went up to the fifteenth floor. So I decide to punch the button again.

Faith then is your decision to respond to God's Word. The decision may either manifest itself in some outward action or else in what we might call an "interior action"—like the committing of your eternal destiny into the hands of Christ. In time the decision grows into an attitude, an attitude of always being ready to respond positively to God's Word.

When I was younger, and more absorbed in faith/science tensions in my studies, I used to point out that faith is a decision or an attitude *based on evidence* (the historical evidence contained in the Judeo-Christian documentation). What I said was true, but my vision was limited. I failed then to see that whereas the scientist looks actively for evidence (at the time of writing I am still engaged in scientific research), the Christian has it trumpeted in his ear all day long. God is active in speaking, in revealing, in bringing his Word to my heart. Therefore I now prefer to say that faith is my response to his initiative.

So far we have seen that faith begins with God. He takes the initiative and I respond. When I respond, a third element comes into being since I have now entered into a relationship with him. Faith (my response) has made that relationship possible. He speaks; I respond; and we begin to get to know each other. And the better I know him the easier I will find it to respond obediently to him.

All this militates against the idea that faith may be a feeling. Faith may be *accompanied* by feelings. When I tell the primitive Eskimo from the far north that when he punches button 15 he will ride skywards, he may have anything but feelings of inner assurance. Yet when he has gone through the procedure several times, he will experience them. But his feelings will have no bearing on whether he gets to the fifteenth floor or not. Whether he pushes the button tremblingly or with buoyant enthusiasm, the result will be the same. This was why I used Martha as an illustration. The resurrection of Lazarus from the dead did not depend on Martha's feelings of faith but on her overt response to the word of Christ.

But there is more we must say about faith. So far all we have considered is what it means to the person who believes. Before we go on to discuss how we may learn to respond to greater demands of the Word (how our faith can be increased), we must look at the purpose and scope of faith.

The Invisible and Hoped For
Faith crosses the chasm into the invisible and hoped for.

Hebrews 11:1 is a widely misunderstood verse about faith. In the RSV it reads, "Now faith is the assurance of things hoped for, the conviction of things not seen."

At first sight, the verse may seem to contradict what I have said about faith not being an inner feeling state. Is it not "assurance"? Is it not "conviction"? Many Bible teachers have in fact taken the verse and used it as a succinct definition of faith, by which we are being taught that faith is a state of being sure or of having a conviction.

To interpret the verse in this way is to ignore its context. The focus of the sentence is elsewhere and to understand the point the writer is making we must know which words to emphasize.

You can decide for yourself whether I am right or not by studying the passage as a Bible study exercise at the end of the chapter. But for the present, let me italicize those words that in my judgment point to its real focus.

"Now faith is the assurance *of things hoped for,* the conviction *of things not seen.*"

The verse addresses itself to the sphere of faith's operation. *Faith is the means by which Christians do business beyond time and space and bring to pass otherwise unrealizable hopes.* Mary's faith made possible the fulfillment of hundreds of years of Jewish longing. It was the means by which the eternal and invisible became mortal and incarnate. Jesus came from beyond outer space through the faith of a peasant girl.

Your own faith then bridges the gap between your humanity and eternity. It can unleash eternal powers here on earth. That is its purpose. You are a bridgehead for the Eternal God in the place where he has put you. The whole might of eternity can pass through you to touch people around you. All you do is obey God.

Because obedience is crucial I must return to it. Faith is not given to you in order that you might become a Christian Mr. Electric. Although God's awesome power is unleashed when you respond to his Word, faith is not a line to the celestial powerhouse which you may hook up to whatever gadgets you choose. Faith and obedience are so inseparable as to be one. God gave you faith that you might be one of his agents. Indeed your faith is but one link in a complex chain of circumstances by which God brings his will to pass. Mary's faith was only one of a vast array of factors involved in God's plan to become incarnate. So you are not to be a magician but something infinitely more exciting—a collaborator with the eternal purpose.

Increasing Your Faith
It may seem that I have been down-playing an emphasis on the amount of faith. And I have. Yet now that we have a clearer understanding of what faith is and of how much can be accomplished with how little, it is time we addressed ourselves to the question of the best way to increase our faith.

But if I have defined faith as man's response to God's initiative, in what terms can I discuss its increase? Either you respond or you don't. Yet the New Testament distinguishes between great faith and little faith. It also talks about *enduring* faith. What do these terms mean?

Strong faith is faith that continues to respond to the Word of God in the absence of outward encouragement. It is the faith of my little dog who sits obediently on the lawn when we go off shopping in the car and is still waiting for us when we return. It is the church's refusal to abandon the hope of Christ's return in spite of the fact that in the first century and in the thirteenth century every indication might have pointed then to his soon return. But he didn't come. He said he would come soon. That was two thousand years ago.

I grope in my mind for contemporary illustrations of this strong (enduring) faith, but I fail constantly. Each time I think I have one, I find that it is not an example of faith, but of a *need* to go on believing. The abandoned wife who refuses to relinquish her belief that her husband will return ("He *said* he would, and I know he won't break his promise"), the children who cling to the Santa Claus myth putting up their stockings even when their friends ridicule them, the belief of the middle-aged person in the goodness of human political institutions, the patronage of the ballot box in the face of every violation of promise and betrayal of trust—these all may exemplify weakness not strength. They are usually the pathetic defense of vulnerable people to the terrible cutting edge of truth. And that is not what I am talking about.

I am talking about Abraham—old dried up Abraham—hobbling to the altar with his strapping manly son and lifting his knife to kill the boy as a sacrifice, believing that the promise made years before would still be fulfilled through this same Isaac however crazy God's immediate instructions might seem. I am talking about what appears to observers as a smiling insanity, yet what is in fact a glorious gamble with a clear-eyed perception both of what the odds appear to be on the surface and of what they really are. I am talking of Paul singing with Silas in jail at midnight or wind-whipped on the deck of a storm-battered ship calming the panicky crew with an assurance that all would be well. These all exemplify an irrevocable commitment, not only to principles, but to the Word of God—come drought, come tornado, come ten feet of snow. This, this ability not to quit obeying whatever may seem to go wrong, this is strong faith. To grow in your capacity to persist like this is to increase your faith.

To put it another way, great faith is responding to God *when it is hardest to do so,* either when the thing he demands of you hurts or else seems to be totally impractical.

My earliest experience of the impractical/impossible instruction occurred while I was in the British Navy at the close of World War 2. We wanted to advertize our Bible study/prayer meetings in the aircraft carrier on which we were returning from the Far East. I knew I had to approach the skipper—a testy, irascible professional—and do the asking.

"What d'yew want?" he asked as I stood to attention in his cabin. "Hurry. I haven't got time to waste. What? Bible study? *I* read the lesson on this ship and we don't need Bible studies."

I stood and waited. There seemed nothing else to do.

"Well? What are you waiting for?"

"I want to put up a notice, Sir. . . ."

"Dammit didn't you hear what I said? *I* take Sunday services on this ship. I read the prayers. I read the lesson. Nothing more is needed."

"Yes Sir."

Silence.

"Why are you still standing there, White? The door is behind you."

I felt sick.

"I want to put a notice up Sir. . . ."

"Damn you, damn you, DAMN YOU. Don't I make sense?" (Pause.) "Put your idiotic notice up. Put up any notice you like. GET OUT!"

"Yes Sir—and thank you very much, Sir."

I am not a hero. But I *did* go into the office. And the whole idea did seem crazy. But some men found Christ as a result and very many were made bolder in their faith.

I'm sorry to go on with theory, but there's something else we must be clear about before we get to "how-tos."

I may have been giving the impression that great faith is rather like great will power. There is a germ of truth in the idea. Faith involves decisions and attitudes both of which are associated with your volition. But faith is not will power and will power is not faith. Faith has to do with a personal relationship. It is faith *in someone*. When I hang on in the face of what seems like meaninglessness, it is not just self-control I am exercising. Self-control plays very little part. I hang on *because I know who has spoken*. I may have misread what he said, but even that is not terribly important. I know him. I know he is not the kind of person to betray my trust or to let me get beyond his help and care.

Emerson once said that faith is the rejection of a lesser fact and the acceptance of a greater. God is the greater fact. Whatever else impinges on my consciousness I know he *is*. I know he cares.

But when you doubt God, you are doubting one of two things about him: his power or his love. Either you doubt he can help you, or else you doubt that he wants to. To doubt the first is absurd and to doubt the second unthinkable. Yet we do both repeatedly.

How may we stop? How may our faith be increased?

There are several Scripture commands having to do with increased faith. You can increase faith by thinking back on your toughest experiences as a Christian; you may do so by becoming better acquainted with Scripture; you may do so by getting rid of excess spiritual and psychological baggage.

Recalling Bad Times

Have you ever noticed how people who experienced the depression years keep harking back to them? They do so with a kind of pride. If you are not irritated by such people, you may be able to observe that the effect of the depression on them was to toughen and strengthen them and that thinking back to the lean years reinforces their resilience.

If you never thought about it, you might expect that positive and beautiful memories would be the ones to increase our faith. I always believed for instance that one or two really dramatic or miraculous answers to prayer would increase my faith immeasurably. Yet it hasn't worked out that way.

Lorrie (my wife) and I have seen some pretty big miracles in our day. We could, I am sure, collaborate on a "believe-it-or-not" book of incredible answers to prayer. Then why don't we write the book? We don't have time. Such a book is low on our priority list because it would only benefit the bookselling business and our own pockets. It might increase people's faith, but they have a Bible full of better miracles. More to the point, the miracles of which I speak *have not increased our faith at all.* We are ashamed to admit it, but yesterday's miracle does not make today's obedience any easier for us.

The first bit of advice the writer to the Hebrew Christians had about increasing their faith was to think back to the tough times in their past (Heb. 10:32-35). Kenneth Taylor translates the passage as referring to "wonderful days," but see what kind of "wonderful days" they were, even in The Living Bible.

Don't ever forget those wonderful days when you first learned about Christ. Remember how you kept right on with the Lord even though it meant terrible suffering. Sometimes you were laughed at and beaten, and sometimes you watched and sympathized with others suffering the same things. You suffered with those thrown into jail, and you were actually joyful when all you owned was taken from you, knowing that better things were awaiting you in heaven, things that would be yours forever. Do not let this happy trust in the Lord die away. Remember your reward!

You would think the writer would have more sense than to remind discouraged Jews of how rough it used to be. After all, it appears from the context that the Jews in question were seriously considering dropping their Christian beliefs. Yet it is precisely to the tough times that he directs their thinking.

Why?

I do not altogether know. Tough times, of course, do one of two things to you. They either break or make you. If you are not utterly crushed by them (in which case you will do all you can to bury their memory), you will be enlarged by them. Their pain will make you live more deeply and expand your consciousness in a way LSD never could. Evidently, the Jews whom the writer addressed had undergone such experiences in their sufferings. God had loomed larger in them. Their experience in Christ proved more exciting. Therefore the memories were pain-wrapped but precious. And when the pain wrappings were taken off and the memories relived, their hearts would be stirred to warm allegiance again. Their faith would be quickened.

If you have only just come to Christ, your rough time may not yet have taken place. But if you've been longer on the way—think back. Remember what happened? How you felt? Doesn't it begin to move you? And aren't you a better person for being stirred in this way? Doesn't a more *solid* sort of faith begin to be rooted?

Think well on the rough times in your Christian past.

Remembering the Promises
"Remember your reward!" says the writer of the Hebrew letter (Heb. 10:35, Living Bible).

Faith is increased as we acquaint ourselves with Scripture. "Faith cometh . . . by the word of God" (Rom. 10:17, KJV). The same mysterious writer of the letter to the Hebrews underscores the point in 12:1, though most translators and commentators miss the point of what he is saying. "Wherefore seeing we also are compassed about with so great a cloud of witnesses . . . let us run with patience (or endurance)" (Heb. 12:1, KJV).

What is he saying? Who are the witnesses? Obviously they must be one of two kinds. The "witnesses" are either *bearing witness to us* or else they are witnesses in the grandstands, watching the race, that is, *witnesses of us.* "Since we have such a huge crowd of men of faith watching us *from the grandstands* . . ." (Heb. 12:1, Living Bible); "With all these *witnesses to faith* around us . . ." (Heb. 12:1, NEB).

Watching us from the grandstands? How depressing. How can I compete with Abraham? Dear old Moses, I know you mean to be encouraging, but did you *have* to come and watch while I go through my miserable performance? (Think how a young pianist would feel if he had to perform before an audience of Paderewski, Chopin, Rubinstein, Van Cliburn and so on.)

Fortunately, the grandstand interpretation of the verse, supported a little by the figure of an athletic event (a race), is not supported by the context as a whole. No, the writer's point is to bring witnesses before us who will testify *that faith is worth it.* Throughout chapter 11 he has been telling us of men and women who under the most incredible circumstances endured in their faith. Now he brings the lesson home to us personally by saying that these same people have been given to bear witness *to* us. They do not watch from the grandstand. They encourage from the starting line.

Herein lies a very important truth about Scripture. It is the Word of God. But it is in the form of the witness of men and women about God, about his faithfulness, about how he sustains those who trust him. (In this sense Hebrews 11 is a microcosm of the whole of Scripture.) These men and women, through Scripture, bear witness to us about the God of the universe. And their witness is meant to be a source of faith to us.

God could have by-passed the witnesses. He could have dictated to someone in a trance. (In fact he did on rare occasions.) But he chose, in the main, to give his infallible Word through the experiences and words of fallible men and women.

In this way the Bible is doubly personal. It is personal in that it is a personal message from God to each one of us. We must study it if we want more faith. But it is also personal in the sense that it is a message from flesh and blood men and women across the centuries to us. By the Spirit these people gather round us in a cloud as we prepare ourselves for the race of faith.

Therefore you must study Scripture in order to grow in faith. Study the lives of bygone "heroes of faith." Discover how human they were and how slow to learn. Modern biographies of outstanding Christians might depress you, whereas the scriptural narrative of the life of an Abraham or of a David will enable you to discover how patient God is in training essentially feeble believers to make them giants of faith.

As you study Scripture, too, other changes will take place in you. The promises of God will sometimes come home to you with peculiar power and sweetness. They will be of enormous help to you as you try to be obedient at times of difficulty. Again, your study will throw light on problems which impeded your faith. The Holy Spirit will clear up at least some of the problems which bothered you as you become better acquainted with the Word of God.

The Christ of the Scriptures will also be food on which your faith will grow. A vision of his strength and power will uplift you for you will begin to discover that the same strength and power are available for you. His endurance in the face of opposition will not only inspire you. You will see it as an endurance he wants to share with you so that it becomes yours.

I referred earlier to the nervousness of the young pianist performing to an audience of masters. But there is a different image. How would the young pianist feel if just before his entrance Rubinstein grabbed his elbow and said, "I know how it feels. I've had some pretty bad times before critical audiences. But stick with it. It's worth it. I'll be rooting for you." Such a young pianist would sit not on a piano stool, but on a cushion of air to play explosions of light and caresses of angels.

And this is your lot. Moses is at your elbow as you approach the starting point. So are Joshua and Rahab the harlot. So too are thousands of unknowns who went through hell on earth and proved God true. They are straining to speak to you, to tell you something; and about someone. . . .

Getting Rid of Excess Baggage
But it's a race all right, a race of faith, a long and gruelling race in which you cannot afford to be weighed down. Unconfessed sin, useless priorities will weaken your faith.

It is easy enough to understand why unconfessed sin will impede faith. I won't go into the matter at this point. But what about the useless priorities?

A Christian is a one-priority-person. Jesus made it clear what his followers had to be. "Ye cannot serve God and mammon," he stated bluntly (Mt. 6:24, KJV). A Christian cannot have a vivid faith if he is torn in two directions at once.

It is precisely here that many Christians fail. Attracted by money or by pleasure, by a career, by position or prestige they try to close their eyes to the fact that human nature makes it impossible for us to have more than one supreme goal in life. Ask them what their supreme goal is and they'll say, "To glorify God, . . . to serve Christ," and so on. But watch their lives and you'll be puzzled. Talk to them and you'll find a strange lack of excitement about the glory of God. You'll also find little evidence of vital faith.

Most of my Christian physician colleagues are doctors first and Christians second. They would be reluctant to admit this and might accuse me of being judgmental. Nevertheless it is a fact, a fact not peculiar to physicians but also true of Christian lawyers, Christian teachers and others. It's even true of Christian garbage collectors—though less true. Garbage collectors tend not to make garbage-collecting their supreme goal in life. They think of themselves as

Christians who happen to collect garbage for a living. Professionals have more of a temptation at this point.

But it is a temptation to be overcome. No man can serve two masters. "He will either hate the first and love the second, or treat the first with respect and the second with scorn" (Mt. 6:24, Jerusalem Bible).

If I think of myself as a psychiatrist who is also a Christian, I am in trouble. When I think of myself as a Christian who also practices psychiatry, I am not only more free to serve Christ, I do a better job at psychiatry. The distinction is not subtle but fundamental. It has to do with goals and loyalties, prime goals and prime loyalties, and with the nature of freedom and slavery. Let a man be honest with himself and so let him run this race; for he that runneth ambivalently runneth his faith into the ground.

The unnecessary weight does not have to be a career goal, however. It can be almost anything—trivial or important. Christian mother, what are you—Christ's follower who is also called to do a good job of mothering or a mother who is also a Christian? When Satan comes to you and says, "Back off on your Christian stand and I will not hurt your child," what do you do?

Christ calls us inflexibly and uncompromisingly to one loyalty. Unless you can identify and ditch competing goals and loyalties, you will never be a man or woman of faith.

Being Tried by Fire
So far we have talked of what *you* can do to increase your faith. To some extent we have ignored what God is doing and how you may cooperate with him.

For the goal of increasing your faith is his goal even more than it is yours. He has been working actively on it since before you became a Christian in ways which, given the preference, you would hardly have chosen for yourself.

As fire refines gold, so "when the heat is on" your dross

will surface, and twenty-four carat faith gradually develop underneath (1 Pet. 1:7). As drought drives the roots of trees deeper underground, so your faith will send her roots downward into the ground of your being in times that seem spiritually dry. And you will be green in drought.

Both fire and drought are part of God's disciplinary process. He trains, disciplines, shapes you as a runner in the race of faith, as a fighter in the warfare of faith. The training involves correction and pain. Your faith will increase or decrease according to how you respond to his intervention.

All the time I have been writing this chapter, a section of the Hebrew epistle (10:32—12:13) has been a backdrop to my thinking. I have resisted the temptation to point to each glittering gem in this remarkable treasure trove so that you might not miss the glory of the whole treasure by being taken up with individual pearls. The section ends by discussing faith as a personal relationship in a family (Heb. 12:5-11).

Faith grows by painful discipline carried out by the father of the family.

There is a fundamental error common to nearly all books (secular and Christian) on child-rearing. To my knowledge no one has ever pointed it out. It matters little whether the theoretical viewpoint of the writer is that of a learning theorist (model, conditioning, and so forth), a Gestalt theorist, an analyst or a scriptural theologian. All seem to fall into the same trap when it comes to child-rearing. They assume that there is an absolute correlation between what the parent does (prays, sets limits, understands) and how the child turns out.

Strange that this absurdly nonsensical idea should persist in the face of all the evidence against it. We are determinists. We have been brainwashed into believing that causes, *some* causes, *somewhere, somehow,* must produce all the "effects." We are worshipers of Aristotle. Our minds are frozen by the fascination and the glorious simplism of cause/effect. It reduces the universe to that which my puny brain can master, and I grow big with confidence. I can explain it all, even the kid who goes wrong.

There *are* causes. There *are* effects. But there is a ghost (and not just the one Koestler described) in the machine. A child is not a programmable computer. ("Of course not," some of my opponents chant, though B. F. Skinner remains silent, "We never said it was. The very idea is horrible." Yet they act like it is true.)

Different children will respond to the same disciplinary "causes" with a variety of "effects." The race is not to the parentally swift nor the battle to the child-rearing strong. The child chooses. He cooperates with the process or he sabotages it. The best parents in the world sometimes produce monsters; while the breakers of every child-rearing rule may produce a family of responsible, adjusted little angels. It happens all the time.

The writer to the Hebrews knows this. He points it out to the Jews who are wavering between belief and unbelief. The Christian Jews can choose what they do about the discipline. God is not a Celestial Programmer.

But in facing their choice they must keep a number of things in mind. First, discipline is an evidence of parental love. To receive no discipline means you are a "love child" rather than a loved child. "When he whips you it proves you are really his child" (Heb. 12:6, Living Bible).

Again they must realize that discipline is painful. It is not "punishment." (I am a little unhappy with the Living Bible and the Jerusalem Bible at this point. Punishment is retributive. Discipline is purposeful training and the context is plainly dealing with the latter.) "Discipline...is never pleasant; at the time it seems painful" (Heb. 12:11, NEB). Criticism from the trainer, gruelling hours of extra exercise, sweat, weariness and pain (both physical and psychological) are all part of the deal for the athlete. Should Christian training, training in the exercise of faith, be any less rigorous?

But the crunch lies in how the Christian responds to the discipline. It is this that determines whether faith will blossom or wither.

Years ago when plastic surgery was less developed than it now is, patients often underwent painful operations to improve their appearance. Some surgeons felt that anesthetics, whether local or general, would interfere with the final result. Carol Lombard, after a car accident in which she received severe facial injuries, was said to have been faced with the choice of severe pain on the operating table or the loss of her beauty. She chose pain.

But the pain itself did not regain her loveliness for her. Two elements combined to do this: the surgeon's skill and Miss Lombard's stillness. Had she been unwilling during the operation to endure pain quietly; had she struggled or twisted her head as the scalpel was cutting or the needle suturing, then the same operation that in fact restored beauty could have produced a disastrous deformity of her features.

"Discipline, no doubt, is never pleasant; at the time it seems painful, but in the end it yields for those who have been trained by it the peaceful harvest of an honest life" (Heb. 12:11, NEB).

For those who have been trained by it. . . . Here is the crux of the matter. You may have the beauty of God's image restored in you by corrective soul surgery. God's tenderness and skill are at your disposal. The knife is poised; the sutures ready. How will you respond? Will you wriggle and squirm? Or will you quietly thank him, not for the pain, but for the process of correction associated with it?

God does not change you by magic. No wand will be

waved over your head so that your deepest problems vanish overnight. There may be breakthroughs, sudden insights, glorious experiences. But the major work of transformation will be slow and often deeply painful. Yet the pain is immeasurably reduced by trust and understanding.

My oldest boy, Scott, was born badly crippled in Bolivia. For the first year of his life he was locked in what looked like brutal splints. (They caused him little or no suffering, however.) When he was a year old the splints were removed, and soon he was running and walking. Inevitably he had his first bad fall, splitting his chin widely with a gash that extended up into the floor of his mouth.

We were far from civilization. I had no surgical instruments, only a pair of eyebrow tweezers and household needles and thread. I had no means of relieving pain. Firm hands gripped his tiny form as I inflicted what must have seemed like unbelievable pain on my terrified son. To say my heart was breaking sounds sentimental, yet his pain was my pain. Why was there no way by which I could comfort him with the knowledge that all would be well? Why did I have to frighten as well as hurt him? I agonized over his ordeal as I gripped his tender skin with eyebrow tweezers and brutally jabbed a sewing needle again and again into his chin.

But I learned two things. First, that God is not a sadist. He takes no pleasure in our pain. If I, a human father, agonized so deeply over the pain I was inflicting on my child, how much more did my Heavenly Father grieve over our sorrows? Isaiah taught this as fact hundreds of years ago. "In all their affliction, he [God] was afflicted" (Is. 63:9, ASV).

I also discovered that although pain is magnified by fear, it is dramatically alleviated by understanding and trust. I could not convey what I was doing to Scott, but God can and does convey it to us. I found that in the midst of the psychological stresses and pains of certain experiences I was undergoing at the time, if only I understood or even, not withstanding, trusted, the pain was turned into joy. Trusting, I became a collaborator with God in the operations by which he remade his image in me and deepened my faith.

In my teens I was taught piano by a superb teacher. "Play anything you want, today," he would sometimes tell me, then listen attentively to my immature productions. When I had finished, he would sit silently, puzzling. After a few minutes he would seize manuscript paper and scribble a few notes on it. "There. Try to play *that*," he would say as he placed the new exercise in front of me.

Always I found it frustrating and difficult to do so. "O.K. Take it slowly at first. Pick up speed when it comes naturally. Try working on it for a week."

Little by little an astonishing technical fluency began to come to my fingers. The hated exercises became stepping stones to musical freedom. I began to take a fierce delight in grappling with whatever exercise in frustration my teacher placed before me.

"Count it all joy," writes James, "when ye fall into divers temptations [that is, trials]; knowing this, that the trying of your faith worketh patience [that is, endurance]" (Jas. 1:2-3, KJV).

It is in this sense that we rejoice in sufferings. We do not do so because suffering is good but because God uses suffering, even when it arises from sin, as an instrument to perfect our faith and to make it tough and enduring. It is possible then not only to have our faith immeasurably increased according to the way we respond to trials but to discover that the pain of the trials can be transmuted into joy. Therefore you must thank God in the midst of your pain. Tell him you trust him. Praise him for what he can do, for what he *is* doing. As you do so pressures will lift. You will be given a garment of praise to replace a spirit of heaviness.

These and other lessons about how my faith could be perfected came home to me climactically one day in Bolivia. Oppressed by what I felt was far more than my share of trials, and feeling myself bereft of human comfort and understanding, I cried to God one Saturday afternoon to give me "just one word of comfort." I asked for a crumb and in the end he gave me a banquet.

Because of the pressures I decided to take the next day (Sunday) off. Lorrie and I would not even attend morning service but would cross the river behind the tiny Bolivian settlement of Tambo and climb through the semi-desert to the top of a steep hill overlooking the river valley.

Some of the pressures slipped away temporarily almost as soon as we had forded the river. God ministers peace through nature. With the sun warming our bodies we climbed between thorny shrubs, giant cactus and kapok trees, helping each other over the steep places and clambering determinedly upwards. The settlement below began to appear like a beautiful toy world. An intense blueness in the sky colored the foam-flecked river below.

Half way up the hill we stopped to rest and to hold our own mini-worship service. We had a Gideon New Testament, and as we sat together we turned to the back of it where one or two hymns were printed. Perhaps God would speak his special word to me now. With no particular thought in mind we selected a hymn and began to sing.

How firm a foundation, ye saints of the Lord,
Is laid for your faith in His excellent word!
What more can He say than to you He hath said,
To you who for refuge to Jesus have fled?

What more can he say than to you he hath said? A bomb went off in my skull. I had been asking for a word and here was God saying that he had already said all that needed saying. I began to cry—for joy and relief. Faith cometh by the Word of God.

Lorrie went on singing.

"When through fiery trials thy pathway shall lie,
My grace, all sufficient, shall be thy supply;
The flame shall not hurt thee; I only design
Thy dross to consume, and thy gold to refine."

So suffering did have meaning. God was doing something through my trial.

"When through the deep waters I cause thee to go,
The rivers of sorrow shall not overflow;
For I will be with thee, thy trial to bless,
And sanctify to thee thy deepest distress."

I will be with thee, thy trial to bless. It was not a cold inhuman process. The warm breath of Aslan was about me and the fragrance of his mane.

"The soul that on Jesus hath leaned for repose,
I will not, I will not desert to its foes;
That soul, though all hell should endeavor to shake,
I'll never, no never, no never forsake!"[5]

I am unclear as to what happened next. I know my nose was running and that Lorrie was being very motherly. But nothing mattered. A radiance far greater than that of the mountain air had broken over me and I felt the strength of ten men. Soon we were climbing upwards again, struggling happily against the downward pull of gravity and the vicious stabs of cactus and thorn bushes.

And in a sense we've been climbing ever since—gravity and thorns notwithstanding.

A Passage to Study
Read Hebrews 10:32—12:13.

1. Hebrews 10:32-39. Faith, enduring faith, may be helped by calling to mind past trials (vv. 32-34). But what evidences are there in these verses that having faith or not having it is something that is placed under my control?

2. Hebrews 11. Pick out those examples in the chapter

which have to do with the "not seen" and the "hoped for," and try to show how the writer illustrates his thesis in verse 1 by the examples that follow.

3. Hebrews 12:1-13. In what way does "looking to Jesus" help our faith? What response are we to make in the midst of disciplinary pain? Are you making that response?

7

Changed Relationships

As a Christian you are a person with two families: a heavenly one and an earthly. In becoming a Christian you began your relationship with the first and changed your relationships in the second. The course of relationships in both rarely remains untroubled. No fights are so fierce as Christian fights and no quarrels so bitter as family quarrels. On the other hand no fellowship can be so warm as Christian fellowship and no shelter so comforting as a home where relationships are what they should be. It is important, then, that we look at both families carefully.

The Biological Family

Recently I was asked to give a seminar on "A Whole Family in a Fragmented World." The seminar was for Christians, many of whom must have assumed that Christianity would knit fragmented families together. And so it may. But equally well, it may create new tensions and clashing loyalties. "Think not that I am come to send peace on earth: I came not to send peace, but a sword," Jesus asserted. "For I came to set a man at variance against his father.... And a man's foes shall be they of his own household" (Mt. 10: 34-36, KJV).

The words are disturbing. The Prince of Peace hammers on the door of your home with the hilt of his sword. This makes us ask the question: What is the Bible's view of the family? Throughout the Old Testament we are made aware of its importance. Does it become less important in the New Testament? Does Christ's coming change matters?

Social workers, marriage counselors, psychoanalysts, family therapists and psychologists all proclaim the importance of the family unit. It is true that voices are raised predicting the doom of the family. But they are lone voices, scarcely heard among the general clamor. As I write, family therapy threatens to become more important in medicine than any other form of psychological treatment. There may be different theories about *how* families function, but there is almost unanimous opinion that function they must, by whatever means we can make them.

Ought not Christians, then, be in the forefront in healing fractured families?

Of course they must. But important as the family is, there are yet more important things. If unity in the family can only exist at the expense of its members' loyalty to Jesus Christ, then the good has become the enemy of the best. You must be loyal to Christ whatever it may cost you *or anyone close to you,* whatever the consequences to your family, your community, your country.

There must be no compromise. Other ideologies (communism, fascism and so forth) have claimed the first loyalty of party members over family and other loyalties. There is only one person who can make so vast a claim—that is the Ruler of the Universe, the Lord of lords and King of kings.

It would be wrong of me to suggest that Christ's aim is to stir up a hornet's nest in your home. God creates institutions to work—not to fall apart. The family is one of *his* institutions.. But sometimes a structure has been so undermined that it needs to be pulled apart and rebuilt before it can stand. Therefore an explosion in a family, however painful it may be, need not dismay you. It may result from a sickness that has been there for years. Or it may represent a clearing of debris that presages a new building.

God, who created the family, designed it to work best when all its members are rightly related to himself. It can, however, function without this: never as well as when he is given his proper place, but surprisingly well, even so, just as a car may function superbly when stolen from its owner or even when some of the manufacturer's instructions are ignored. (That the car should do so is a tribute to the manufacturer's competence but in no way justifies either the car's theft or careless treatment.) So non-Christian families can still function well.

There may be difficulty when you let the folk at home know about your relationship with Christ. Tensions may increase if you are loyal to your new Master. But be clear about one thing. Tensions may increase, but it must never be your aim to increase them. Anger may come, but you must never seek to stir it up. Making and breaking families is God's business, not yours. And the breaking of a family is always a tragedy—even when God, in mercy, has to do it.

In no place must you watch your attitude more carefully than in your own family. Christians tend to be a little self-righteous at home, new Christians especially so. Beware of "righteous indignation" about the sins of other family members. Show others the same mercy and patience that Christ showed you. Do you feel that your family has had all the mercy it deserves? Well, so had you, long before God got through to you.

I am beginning this chapter, then, with a word both of caution and of reassurance: of *reassurance*, because any feeling of hesitation you have about telling your family about

Christ is understandable; of *caution* first, because however kindly and tactfully you confess your allegiance to Christ, the news may be received coldly or even lead to alienation, and second, because you must beware of becoming the family prig.

Things may turn out well. You may find the whole family prepared by the Holy Spirit and hungry for truth. This happens. The whole family may turn to Christ and believe.

More commonly, however, the immediate results are less pleasing. The acceptance of your confession will most likely differ from one family member to another. A spouse may be deeply moved and a parent or a child rejecting. Or a spouse may be alienated and children or parents listen with eager acceptance.

New constellations of intra-family alliances may make their appearances and you must be on the watch for them. It is not your job to line up supporters for the Christian cause as though you were campaigning for Christ in the family. Any support you get from one family member may threaten and hurt another. If Christ brings about a new relationship of warmth and solidarity between my sister and me, I must be sensitive to the hurt and alienation of my younger brother who was once my sister's bosom companion. Christ would not have me gloat about my conquest but rather have me suggest to my sister that she not forget the needs of the brother with whom she was once so close.

Your job then is to be a center of truth, of love and of light in your home. This does not require you to be unnatural. Christ has lit a light in your heart. Be yourself in your family, but let that self belong to God.

The Family: A Script to Follow, a Score to Dance
The family, however much we may wish to change it, remains at its healthiest only when its members relate as God designed them to relate. It was designed to function neither

as a democracy nor as a dictatorship nor yet as an economic unit in an agrarian society. Social change may modify its size or its links with the rest of the world, but nothing has and nothing ever will alter its essential nature.

Families exist because God designed humans to live in families. And whatever futurologists may say to the contrary, the moment man ceases to live *en famille* he will cease to be distinctly man, to become less human and more ant-like. I make this statement on biblical rather than scientific grounds. All science can say (whether the sciences of anthropology, sociology or psychology) is what *is* happening to families and what *might* happen to them. Science can never say what *ought* to happen since science has no way of knowing what a *normal* family is. It can only know what a *usual* family *seems* to be like in a given cultural setting. Normality lies beyond the bailiwick of science. It implies purpose and design of which science knows nothing.

God is not a bachelor; he is a Trinity.

Whatever way we may conceive or fail to conceive in the nature of the Trinity, of one thing we may be sure. Human beings did not invent it out of their neurotic need for security. People who say that *man* created *God* as a father forget this. God, as he is revealed to us, comes not just as Father, but as a Three-in-One, an entity which we cannot understand let alone invent.

However, he *is* revealed to us as Father; and man, created in his image, is created also with an innate capacity for intimate personal relationships. The family unit may well meet basic biological needs. It may correlate with certain cultural and economic conditions, but these needs and conditions are less basic than we suppose. The family unit arises out of what God is in the very core of his being.

The God who created man made the basics of family relationships explicit. To be God's servant in your family involves living out your special role (of child, wife, parent or whatever) as it is conceived in the inspired script. There is no more powerful way than this of bearing witness to your family or of being God's agent of change and of healing there. And remember, your role, whatever it may be, does not include that of general judge and critic.

Long before I ever became a psychiatrist, I found myself involved in what is now known as family counseling. Because I was familiar with the biblical script for family role-playing, I would frequently point out to a father, a husband or a wife exactly what the script called for. Very soon I became accustomed to a stock reaction which in summary ran something like this: "Yes, I know the Bible says I ought to love my wife, but it also says she should obey me. And she doesn't. I'll start playing my part when she starts playing hers."

I call this the "Yes—But" Response, and with slight word changes it can be placed in the mouth of any family member. In essence it pleads that one cannot be expected to fulfill one's role in the family properly unless every other member of the family is fulfilling theirs.

I hesitate to dismiss the protest out of hand. Yet you can see at once that it forms an impossible basis for family living. If each family member must first make sure about the satisfactory role-playing of all other family members, or even of any one of them, the home becomes a forum for endless bickering. Commitment of each member to the unit becomes tentative and fragile. No stability is possible. And the essence of family relationships is that they be, like God's relationship with us, based on unswerving commitment. It is the solid unconditional commitment of family members to one another that makes the growth of rich personal relations possible. (Unfortunately it does not guarantee them.)

This then must form the foundation stone of your relationship to your family. There must be a solid, unswerving commitment to God to play whatever your role may be in the family for his sake and without any regard to how well other family members play theirs. This is part of your Christian commitment. The others may reject you. The family as a whole may turn you out. But until it does, you are committed to God's script for father, son, wife, mother, husband or whatever. Even if the family throws you out, you should be ready at the drop of a hat to resume your role.

Each role is played in relation to other roles. Or, to change the image from a play to a ballet, you do not pirouette in isolation. In the conjugal pas de deux, while there must be submission by each dancer to the other, the principal steps for the husband are those of love and sacrifice while those of the wife are of submission and reverence (Eph. 5:21-33). The steps must be rehearsed constantly if a beautiful performance is to take place.

Much of the unpopularity of the score arises because we bring our rigid and barren twentieth-century thinking to bear on it. We confuse equality with sameness, and while apparently asking for the one, in reality we are asking for the other. The result is not a pas de deux, but a non-dance —drab, grey and unsatisfying.

Or else the dancing is competitive, each in the conjugal dance vying to take over the more desirable steps from the other. Understandably, the partners frequently come to grief—now tangling and tripping ungracefully, now soaring to crash from empty space where welcoming arms should have been.

Let me be more concrete. God does not make the husband responsible for the wife's submission or the wife responsible for the husband's love. Each is to follow the score that is written for him or her. If the other member of the pas de deux fails, it is the joint responsibility of the choreographer and producer to deal with the matter.

Therefore leave God with the responsibility of dealing with your partner's failure. Concentrate on your own steps. If you are a husband, love and sacrifice. Do so in the face of disappointment. If you are a wife, dance the dance of submissive reverence with beauty and dedication as long as you can go on doing so. If you are a son or daughter, honor your parents. And unless obedience to parents constitutes disobedience to Christ, be obedient. If you say, "If you knew my parents, you wouldn't talk about honoring them," you are playing the "Yes—But" game. Honor them because though they may do a poor job at representing God, they do in fact do so. Honor them also because you now belong to Christ, and this is what he would have you do.

I could go through the roles of father, mother, child and so forth according to the biblical score. But I think you can see what I am getting at. You might ask, "Is not the whole business a masochistic exercise in futility?"

Even if it were, we should still dance by the score. Yet to do so is not masochistic, for often it is an experience in joy, not in pain. And as for being futile, it can produce powerful effects. We may not be trained dancers, but we can be compared with them in that there is something deep within a family relationship that is analogous to the feeling of a dancer who responds to a fellow dancer performing his or her part perfectly. There is a stirring within our limbs to respond to the perfection and beauty of what we see and to be drawn into the dance for sheer wonder. Bitterness and rebellion slowly melt away and our feet come to life. Therefore when you dance with skill and vigorous abandon, I begin to feel an inner pull. It may take you some time to get my feet tapping, but I cannot deny the urge that is within me (1 Pet. 3:1-2).

Yet whether other feet are stirred to dance or not, the choreographer has written a score for you. Dance it. Your temptation will be to indulge in fantasies about the kind of family you would like to have around you. Such fantasies may well be turned into prayer, and it could be that much of the frustration in your family life springs from the fact that you have one program that you are striving for while God has another. *It is not God's prime aim to make your family nice for you to live with.* He may even want you to learn lessons about making things easier on them. Or his plans may encompass things you never dreamed of.

Jacob was a bitter and hurt father. Whether he had contributed to the jealousy his sons felt of Joseph is not for us to judge. His favoritism seems to have been shown very unwise. When the whole matter ended in tragedy and when still later his second favorite, Benjamin, seemed doomed to be snatched from him too, we might well say Jacob got what he deserved. But he was in pain. Where was God?

Jacob could not have conceived in his wildest dreams how Joseph would save nations from starvation. From jealousy, murderous hatred and cupidity God had woven a master plan for millions. And in it all, mysteriously, the family itself was restored to harmony.

I cannot promise your family tragedies will prove to be the salvation of western civilization, but I do know God has plans that are wider than your family unit. I also know he brings good out of evil and that he cares about your frustrations and hurts. Don't cling rigidly, therefore, to any set plan of your own about the family's future. Leave the future with God and trust him.

In the meantime you have a score to learn and a dance to dance.

The Family of God

You are a member of the Family of God.

You were cleansed by the same blood, regenerated by the same Spirit. You are a citizen of the same city, a slave of the same master, a reader of the same Scriptures, a worshiper of the same God. The same presence dwells silently in you as in them.

Therefore you are committed to them and they to you. They are your brothers, sisters, your fathers, mothers and children in God. Whether you like or dislike them, you belong to them. You have responsibilities toward them that must be discharged in love. As long as you live on this earth, you are in their debt. Whether they have done much or little for you, Christ has done all. He demands that your indebtedness to him be transferred to your new family.

There is stability in commitment. To have to make too many choices in life renders us anxious and ill at ease. There are areas in our lives where God has taken choice away—not to enslave us, but to set us free from fussing and to liberate us to make creative choices.

We are not allowed to choose our brothers and sisters or whether we shall be committed to them or not. They belong to us and we to them. We have no control over the fact that we are to love, care and be responsible for them. We may fail to live up to our commitment and rebel against Christ. But our rebellion does not abolish the commitment. It will be there as long as life shall endure.

You are committed to *all* your new brothers and sisters. While to some you will be attracted, by others you will be repelled. With some you will discover an instant affinity. There will be a spontaneous warmth and a pleasure in their company. But others will repel you. You will find yourself avoiding them, being irritated by them or else having no feelings at all about them except boredom.

But you are not to confine yourself to the favorite few. You are committed to the freaks and oddballs of the lunatic fringe as well as to those Christians about whom you feel highly critical. You belong to people whose views you disagree with.

It is better so. Where commitment is based on attraction,

it is as temporary as the attraction. It is not, in fact, commitment at all. A relationship bound together by mutual attraction will prove an unstable relationship. More to the point, the parties to such a relationship knowing this are compelled to work at being attractive. The moment they fail to be attractive enough, they may alienate the people who matter to them. Far from being a haven in which to take refuge, then, relationships based on attraction become a source of anxiety and strain.

Women's magazines in the 1960s reflected the "attraction view" of the marriage relationship. Come supper time, wives were encouraged, having tidied the house during the day, to play the warm welcoming siren. Each was to hold on to her husband by listening to his complaints, taking his shoes off, loosening his necktie, feeding him steak with candlelight and wine, and by making sure the children didn't disturb the soft background music. The Japanese geisha was the model for the ideal wife of the 1960s. The rise of the women's liberation movement is understandable.

There is one thing to be said for relationships based on attraction. In whatever way they may fail, they keep you working at being nice to other people. For similar reasons, good hotel chains preserve their clientele by training employees to be courteous to guests. Clerks in exclusive stores still behave as though the customer is always right, and to this day they succeed in making the rich and fussy throw their money away with sighs of contentment.

But you can see at once that there must be better ways of making people work at being kind. If I am kind to you (or attractive to you) only because I want you to go on liking me or because I want your business, then my kindness is phoney. We need real kindness to surround us not commercial or neurotic kindness. We need *loving* kindness based on commitment.

You need it yourself. Somewhere in this world you need

a body of people who will always accept you and always care for you whether you are attractive or not. If you sin, they may rebuke you. They may demand that you repent or put something right. But they will never disown you, never abandon you and never stop caring. Their commitment to you is not based on their admiration for you but on the more solid ground of Christ's person and work.

So when Christ demands you commit yourself to an enduring responsibility toward people you may not naturally care for, he is really doing you a favor. He is insisting that you facilitate the very thing you need, a caring community whose members never fail one another.

But where, you may ask, is such a community to be found?

It already exists and you are a part of it. It is not as though God asks you to start from scratch and build such a community from nothing. There already is a community of saints, bound together by blood, by water, by spiritual life and by the power of God. The fact that its members sometimes fail to live up to their commitment does not destroy the community. It is there. It will not go away. And your relationship with it is something God takes with utter seriousness.

Finding a Church Home

So far I have only stated the matter in general terms, but now we must be practical. How can your responsibility to God's people be worked out from day to day? Take church membership for instance. Let me mention some down to earth principles.

If you do not already belong to a church, try to find one where God's Word is honored and taught clearly and helpfully. It is my personal conviction that the matter of denomination matters less than the health of the local congregation. Ask advice from Christian friends you can trust. Pray about the matter. When you select a church, attend it for several weeks and try to get to know people there. Make a point of introducing yourself to the pastor.

Don't be in a hurry to join until you are sure you are making the right decision. On the other hand don't expect the church to be free of faults and inconsistencies. Few local congregations are. If you are looking for the ideal church, you will look for a long time.

Remember that if the people who attend the church belong to Christ, they are your brothers and sisters. The presence of God the Holy Spirit is in their midst. Some members may have irritating peculiarities. Yet who are you to take offense when Christ has received them? In joining a local congregation you are joining a group of sinners on whom God has had mercy, just as he had mercy on you. The church is not a country club.

If you should already be a member of a church, think about the matter long and hard before changing. Perhaps you have recently come to Christ. If so it is understandable that you should view your church through different eyes. If you belong to a church where Christian conversions take place regularly and where provision is made to help those who are embarking on a new life, there will be no problem. On the other hand you may get the feeling that in your church people will not understand and may not even approve your new found joy.

Beware of sudden moves. You may find, as you listen with awakened ears and watch with enlightened eyes, that there were things going on in your local church that you had never been aware of. You may find others who share your experience of Christ or that the pastor is longing for someone like you to come along. Therefore pray that God will enable you to find any true Christian fellowship that may be available in the church.

Don't become either an instant pharisee or set yourself

up to be martyred and misunderstood. Pray that God will give you an appropriate opportunity to share your new faith with someone in the church. Ask the minister for half an hour of his time and explain to him as clearly as you can what has happened to you. Should you find yourself treated defensively or in an amused patronizing manner, don't rush off in a huff. God will show you, in time, what he wants you to do. It may be that you will need to find a church where the fellowship and teaching you crave are available. Or it may be that God will require you to remain in a struggling church where a faithful few are being used by him to bring revival and new life.

In any event, make sure you find some group of Christians inside or outside the church with whom you can pray and study the Scriptures. Meet regularly with them. Try to look on the weekly experience not as *an activity you have joined* but as *a body of people to whom you belong.*

Be on the look out for ways in which you can help other members of the group. Does someone need a ride? Has someone missed a meal because of shortage of funds? Does someone need a job? Is someone distressed about a personal problem and in need of special prayer? Remember, Christians must be a caring family. Be willing to accept care, and be even more on the alert to give it.

You may have come to Christ through an interdenominational agency (Inter-Varsity, Young Life, Christian Business Men's Committee or another). If this is the case, they will provide a prayer and Bible study group you can attend. A small fellowship-prayer-Bible-study group cannot be stressed enough. Whatever else you have to cut out, don't cut this out. You were meant to grow and develop spiritually *as part of a body* and in fellowship with others.

On the other hand I want to stress with equal force the need for you to belong to a church. The time will come when you will leave the area where you now are or when you may have outgrown the level of fellowship you find in the interdenominational group. In any case it can never serve as a substitute for a local church.

Christ died that humans of every type be reconciled to God and to one another. The genius of Christianity is that it makes possible ongoing fellowship between people who could not otherwise tolerate, let alone enjoy one another. Christ gets refined socialites hobnobbing with migrant farm workers; middle-aged squares weeping with rebels and swingers; blacks, Indians, Jews and wasps praying earnestly together, and management and labor sharing each other's problems. In a world divided by class, commerce, race, education, politics, the generation gap and a million clashing interests, Christ alone can make incompatibles mesh.

So you must never let special Christian activities or interests become a substitute for church fellowship. Of course it is easier to form a comfortable clique of people of your own age and approximately the same outlook. Nor would I disparage the fellowship you experience. It is God-given. Enjoy it and give him thanks. But it may be less remarkable than you think. You could perhaps have experienced almost the same degree of fellowship with the same group without Christ at all if, for example, you all had to survive in a lifeboat after a storm. Christ alone can bring opposites into harmony and the local church is where he delights to do it. What is unique about enjoying the company of someone you like and who shares your background? Members of bridge clubs do the same. I want to return to this point a little later.

Too Many Meetings

You can attend too many meetings. Christian students often excuse neglected studies on the grounds that they were "doing the Lord's work." Husbands neglect their wives and families for the same reason. Important as meetings are, you can misuse them. *They can serve as an escape from less congenial duties.* And tragically, where Christian gatherings serve as an escape, they lose their spiritual value. God wishes us to confront reality, not to escape from it.

For the Christian each task has its appointed place. It is wrong to speak of meetings as being more important than study or than spending time with one's wife or family. No duty is in and of itself more important than any other. You might say on a particular day and for particular reasons (say, if you were going for a job interview), "Shining my shoes is more important than breakfast." But the statement would hardly serve as a general guide for living. Similarly you would not as a general rule take the attitude that it was more important that you eat breakfast than that you get dressed. Eating, washing, sleeping, dressing, exercise, recreation, all have their place in a normal life. Each in its place is equally important. You will devote more time to some activities than to others, but you will (or you should) perform each as well and as zealously in its proper place.

I do not argue that you must not have priorities. There has to be some way of deciding what you include in your life and what you will drop from it, as well as how much time you will allot to what. But having decided (and decide you must), then do each thing well and for the glory of God.

God does not gauge spirituality by the number of meetings you attend or how much time you devote to a Christian friend. He is more concerned with the spirit in which you tackle each duty. Therefore think carefully about how much time you spend in "Christian" activities. Make sure you never use them as an escape from less congenial duties. As a Christian you are to give *all* you do, everything you've got.

The We/They Dichotomy

Considering all the divisions that have plagued Christendom for two thousand years, it is amazing that God has continued to use the church to extend his kingdom. To this day covert battles are raging, hostilities and suspicions fermenting and breeding. Loudly touted church unions patch outward differences while discontent and bitterness seethe within. And for every amalgamation in one place there will be a couple of break-ups some place else.

What can you do about it?

The first thing you must not do is to let the situation throw you. Christ is still in control and he knows what he is doing. His kingdom is advancing. His plans are ripening. No sinful strife evades his watchful eyes. What may cause you to be appalled and deeply discouraged, may grieve but never dismay him. Nothing can or will slow down his forward thrust to final victory and judgment. One day he will root up and fling away many fences that divide his people. Therefore adopt his perspective. Raise your head above dismaying pettiness of local strife and share his victorious stance. As a soldier of Christ you cannot afford to grow cynical and disillusioned.

The next thing is to decide what responsibility you have for the situations you know about. They are of two kinds which may overlap but which can be referred to as big hassles and small hassles. When I talk about big hassles, I am referring not to the heat or fierceness of the divisions, but to the number of people involved. Big hassles involve whole churches, whole denominations or Christian organizations. The fires of the initial strife may have settled down. The organizations concerned may have cooled to slumber alongside each other like sleeping volcanoes, spitting fire only occasionally and half-heartedly.

Obviously you will do well not to monkey around trying to amalgamate sleeping volcanoes. The difficulty is that the "volcanoes" consist of people, many of them Christian people and sooner or later you will adopt an attitude toward them.

As a small boy I used to feel that Catholics were especially wicked and highly dangerous people. I had an aunt who was a Catholic, but I gathered that somehow she wasn't as wicked as most and that though it was all very embarrassing and socially difficult, she was kind of O.K. I liked her but felt uncomfortable in her presence since she was involved in what to me was an esoteric and wicked cult. After all, I knew that the Pope was the antichrist.

I belonged to a small Brethren assembly. We saw ourselves as a highly select group of the elect surrounded both by ordinary sinners and by various kinds of religious or churchgoing sinners. The view was not altogether invalid since in those days in England, church attendance was not a sign of living faith in Christ. The old liberal theology was widely preached.

As I grew older, however, I learned that the view from the bosom of my local assembly was both oversimplified and a little paranoid; but it has taken me years to settle down to what may constitute a wise and godly attitude to Christians of other groups and traditions.

So often I have been among evangelical groups who are obsessed with what I will call the *We/They Dichotomy*. *They* refer to the members of another Christian group. *They* are always the same; that is to say they can be predicted to act in a certain way, to say certain things, to hold identical views and to share identical errors. *Their* characters are remarkably similar. *We* on the other hand, in addition to being right, all have different characters. Some of us are more spiritual than others; we tend to have different strong points. We complement one another's strengths and weaknesses. *We* are human. *They*, in contrast, are stereotypes.

I never really saw my aunt as a person. I saw her through

the distorted windows of my prejudice. In the same way we tend to view Christians and non-Christians alike, not as they really are, but through prejudicial filters that distort their images. It may be that we are afraid. Truth is very important. Our grasp of it is feeble. It bolsters our courage to protect ourselves from being intellectually or spiritually ravished. So we dehumanize and stereotype *them* in our minds in order to render them less threatening and ourselves less vulnerable.

Now there is nothing wrong about knowing you are right. By all means hold on to the truth firmly. Indeed, you need never be afraid that anyone will take it away from you. The truth is a person. He will never leave you nor forsake you. Therefore be zealous to proclaim it and him.

You may have little occasion to meet people of other organizations and traditions. In any case, they too may share the fearful tendency to view the world through We—They spectacles, and may view *you* as threatening, deceived and dangerous. But don't play the same game. Remember that people on the other side of a religious fence are still people. They may even be Christians. Circumstances may make it impossible for you to spend much time together. In any case if your time together is spent in involved discussions about who is right and who is wrong, you may both be wasting your time.

So have a courteous and respectful attitude towards them. Remember they have hopes, problems, fears just as you do. Share anything about Christ that you can without trying to lure them over the dividing fence. Then leave to Christ the matter of the hassle that raised the fence for which neither you nor your acquaintance is responsible.

But it is the small hassles, not the big ones, that will render you a casualty in the warfare against the powers of hate: the hassles inside the local church or the fellowship groups to which you belong. You find yourself irritated by the smugness and patronizing attitude of brother Smith. You feel vaguely guilty about your critical feelings, but then Mr. Smith *is* smug and *is* patronizing. Are you supposed to wear blinkers? Again, Miss Kalansky has been criticizing you behind your back. You resent her. What are you supposed to do? Forgive her? Talk to her?

Let's say your Inter-Varsity group is divided on a doctrinal issue. Feelings are running high. Your doctrinal views are with one party yet you sense that the whole matter has less to do with doctrine than with bruised egos. What should you do?

We could examine each of the common situations I have mentioned or a dozen others you are already familiar with. I would prefer, however, not to discuss how to cope with hassles, but how to take a positive approach and ask: How may we promote unity among God's people? Earlier I mentioned the importance of commitment and closeness among Christians of widely differing background. Yet I said little about how such closeness may be achieved in practice or about the dangers of seeking fellowship as an end in itself.

The Heart of Christian Fellowship

There is more to Christian fellowship than commitment, human closeness or even heterogeneity. You can get a wonderful feeling of being accepted for your naked self from therapy groups and encounter groups. You can experience esprit de corps and comradeship in a wartime military unit. Many of us from Europe have known what it is to survive a night of terrible bombing in a bomb shelter with a strange assortment of people who had been dragged from the rubble of crumpled buildings. As dawn breaks and guns and bombs are silenced, you look at one another with new eyes. Differences are forgotten. You share together the miracle of being alive. You feel you know one another as you have never before known anyone and would serve one another gladly. The experience of "fellowship" is intense, uplifting, humbling even though it is not Christian.

What is it, then, that distinguishes Christian fellowship from every other form of closeness, oneness, togetherness or whatever? Why is it so important that its uniqueness be experienced when so many psychological substitutes are available? What makes truly Christian fellowship so difficult, yet so vital to achieve?

For many Christian writers the heart of the matter lies in the Greek word *koinonia*, a word which has become a theological cliché. You may never have heard it—but no matter. Koinonia is a New Testament word that has to do with sharing something. The something you share may be a material object like a fishing boat (some of the apostles had koinonia in a boat, that is, they jointly owned it) or an experience of Christ.

A sort of mystique has developed around the word, almost as though pronouncing it or understanding its etymology produces Christian fellowship. But you can talk koinonia till the cows come home and never discover what Christian fellowship is about.

The capacity to experience fellowship (to share, to be close, to know) was given by God to all men but was mutilated by sin. Sin has damaged our capacity to know one another because it damaged our capacity to know God. Therefore any attempt to mend the broken fragments of humanity, however exciting or apparently successful, will be illusory and doomed to ultimate failure unless humanity's relationship with God is restored.

I cannot have true fellowship with you unless both of us have fellowship with God. I can love you, feel close to you, enjoy your emotional support. But sooner or later the thing will go sour or remain too shallow to satisfy. Unless both of us experience the healing and reconciling of God through

Christ, unless both of us are restored to an ever deepening relationship with God, then anything we have going between us will be a mere echo of the real thing.

The heart of the matter does not lie in *sharing* (koinonia). It is not that some people share a love of music while we share Christ. If sharing were the crucial point it really would not matter too much *what* we shared. The relationships arising from whatever was shared would be comparable.

But the results are not comparable. At the heart of Christian fellowship is reconciliation, the restoration of your relationship to God. For you can only truly know someone else through God and in God. All other knowing is at least partially illusory.

And your relationship with God is an ongoing thing. It involves what John calls "walking in light" (1 Jn. 1:3-7), that is, maintaining that restored relationship with God by allowing the Holy Spirit to point out your sin and failure, and responding accordingly. As the miracle of the eternal reconciliation is daily renewed in your experience, so too your capacity to have Christian fellowship with another brother or sister will be enhanced.

Here then is the heart of Christian fellowship. It does not have to do primarily with our relationship with one another but rather with our common relationship to God. It is only *in him* that we are one. It is only by making our relationship *with him* primary that our relationships with one another will be what they should be. We cannot be reconciled to another unless we are reconciled to him. Nor can we truly be reconciled to him unless we also be reconciled to (forgiving toward) one another.

Making It Work
True Christian fellowship, then, will be an outworking of a restored relationship with God. It will arise naturally and

spontaneously where my relationship with God is healthy. On the other hand, where you and I fail to experience fellowship, our failure will serve as a sensitive barometer indicating that one or both of us have an impaired relationship with God.

But the fact that we fail to get along does not necessarily mean that each of us should fly to his secret chamber and spend an hour in prayer. There is often no call to pray; the solution may be plain if both of us will only see it. If, for instance, it is my duty to forgive you, there is no need to pray for guidance. I must forgive. That is all there is to it. Even to pray for strength to forgive may be a subtle way of postponing forgiveness.

The rules for maintaining Christian fellowship are simple but tough. You will find them in several parts of the New Testament. Just now I have Philippians 2:3-4 mainly in mind.

Let nothing be done through strife or vainglory (KJV).

What motivates you in the activities of your Christian group? How much of it is either competitive or an attempt to win approval? In the early days, probably little. It is only as time goes on and you find yourself carving a niche in your church or Christian group that the temptation will come. Strife: the word in the context implies the wish to insist on your way because you resent someone else. Your proposed action may be right in itself. But what makes you push it so hard? Does Joe get under your skin and do you sense that he will oppose it? Or do you pursue the matter because of Mary's tendency to steamroller her wishes over everyone else's?

Let nothing be done through strife. Joe's and Mary's ideas may be wrong and their spirit inappropriate. But to fight them with their own weapons is to destroy fellowship. You mustn't fight them at all. The real enemy is the Sower of Discord, and to fight him you begin by putting right your feelings of strife towards Joe and Mary. Having done so, you ask God whether you are really right as to what you thought God wanted. If you are, God may require that you stand firm on your ideas. But standing firm must never be due to your feelings towards Joe or Mary.

Now I know that it is easier for me to write this than for you to carry it out. You may even say that it is impossible for you to feel any other way about Joe and Mary. But you would be wrong. Difficult, I agree, but not impossible. God never tells us to do what is impossible.

The problem of coming to grips with your feelings about Joe and Mary is that it will involve pain for you. To sacrifice resentment is to murder your darling child. It becomes easier when you recognize that Joe and Mary have their own hang-ups and insecurities that call for compassion rather than resentment. It also helps to realize that God cares tenderly for Joe and Mary in spite of what you see as their undesirable qualities.

Therefore lay your resentful feelings on the altar and offer them up in praise to God. Whenever you catch yourself indulging in fantasies of triumphing over Mary or putting Joe in his place, bind your fantasies to the same altar and give them the same treatment. Ruthlessly. Promptly. Always.

Stick with your point if you're sure of it but without riding it to death. If other people buy Joe's and Mary's schemes, don't sulk. God can afford to wait. Be a cheerful dissenter and someone who disagrees courteously and charitably.

Let nothing be done through strife *or vainglory*. You must do nothing in the group with the idea of exciting admiration. Have you discovered a contribution you can make? Something you excel at? Have praises been whispered in your ear? Is there someone else who is not as competent as you? *Let nothing be done through vainglory*. It kills fellowship.

Do nothing from selfishness or conceit, but in humility count others better than yourselves (Phil. 2:3).

So there's something you're good at. Of course you recognize you have your weaknesses. In fact sometimes you feel low. But you're not the lowest man on the totem pole. Would you say you're around the halfway mark? Or higher?

In the quotation I made, Paul poses an intellectual problem. How can most of us "esteem others better than" ourselves? Can we do so and remain intellectually honest? After all, we cannot *all* be the *most* inferior. That unhappy position belongs to only one of us. The rest of us range somewhere between the best and the worst. Would it not be more honest to assess yourself realistically in terms of your place in the scale of values?

By all means be realistic; but what are you measuring when you assess your worth over against Cynthia's? Your scholastic achievement? Your athletic ability? Your clothes? Your body's appearance? Your "personality"? Your spiritual knowledge? Your enthusiasm about Christian things? Your years of experience? Some aggregate of all of these?

For which one of these can you take any personal credit? If they are God-given things, they do not make you *better* than Cynthia only *more fortunate*. They should be a cause of humble gratitude. And if you have been diligent and *can* take credit for something (or think you can), it may be worth less than you think. Human efforts rate low in the divine scale of values.

Do you enjoy the elevation of your position? Are you a president or treasurer or a secretary or even a committee worker? You may stand on a pedestal without being a centimeter taller. The president is still you.

Paul's position is an existential rather than an intellectual one. In discovering the gifts and virtues of others, he has been awed and overwhelmed. He realizes that the question of who is the better man is complex. But in any case it is irrelevant to him. He is more impressed by the gifts of others than by his own.

My father-in-law is a Nova Scotian fisherman. He lacks my years of university training. I could talk more impressively than he on world events, philosophy, the limitations of the scientific method and on and on. My vocabulary is vastly greater than his.

But let us put out to sea in a sailing boat off the rocky coast of Cape Breton. He seems by instinct to know the depth of the water everywhere. In an uncanny way he can find any port within two hundred miles in a fog without navigational aids. I become a stupid landlubber, helplessly inept and out-classed by this sea-taught marvel of a man.

Moreover when he visits my home he wanders around noting what needs to be fixed. I am clumsy with tools, bewildered in the face of practical jobs. He fixes my lopsided garden gate. What to me was a formidable difficulty is to him an afternoon's recreation.

Am I a better man than he? By what scale are the two of us to be measured?

Who can say which of us is *morally* superior? I can quote the Bible more helpfully and people are often moved when I preach in public. Through my own prayers and ministry he recently came back to God after years of wandering. Yet now his joy in Christ and in the Scriptures makes me ashamed. He seems to have progressed more in a few months than I in years. With none of the Bible training or helpful influences to which I have been subjected, he has come far. I stand rebuked before him.

Who will assess us and tell us which of us is the better man before God?

If I go into the presence of God, the question hangs in the air like an obscenity. I know I have done wrong even to ask it. As the majesty of God fills my vision, all questions of human greatness become pointless. I bend my knees. I fall on my face. I tremble and weep with marvel that such a God calls me his child. I am ashamed by my pettiness, my meannesses, my silly deceits and my ugly greeds—yet simultaneously aware that I am forgiven, wanted, loved. How can I go from God's presence asserting my superiority over my brethren? I count myself happy to be the least of them all.

Do you have problems holding other Christians to be better than yourself? If so, pray that God will reveal his greatness and his grace to you. Wait in his presence saying, "My soul, wait thou only upon God." Continue the practice for months—for the rest of your life if need be. And as you see him and see yourself before him, you will have no problem esteeming your brothers better than yourself. You won't crawl. You won't even feel inferior. You will just rejoice in God—and in the wonder of what he is doing in people around you. And in thus rejoicing you will fulfill a basic condition of Christian fellowship.

Let each of you look not only to his own interests, but also to the interests of others (Phil. 2:4).

I am excited about my new car. When people give admiring comments after church, I am gratified. I launch into an account of how I came to make such a good buy. But I am bored when Tom interrupts to tell me that *he* got a good buy on *his* car when he bought it six months ago. Doesn't Tom realize that his car is of no interest to me? Can he be aware how dull his conversation is? I steer the talk firmly back to the marvels of my own acquisition. . . .

I pass through deep waters emotionally. Suddenly in the midst of my trouble God breaks through. A new insight turns my darkness to day, my groaning to joy. In the fellowship meeting I share what has happened with my brothers and sisters who praise God with me for it. But Bill seizes the opportunity to tell everybody about how God has met *his* need during the week. I feel it would be improper not to let him have his say, but I feel restless as the interest of the group turns from me to Bill. To cover my restlessness I join the chorus of thanksgiving for what God has done for Bill. But my heart is not in the matter. My problems and blessings seem vastly more important than Bill's. The fellowship meeting has suddenly gone flat.

Why is it so hard for me to be interested in Bill's joys and sorrows? Can it be that I am looking to my fellow Christians for something I should really look to God for? It is true that God gave me their fellowship partly for my comfort, but perhaps I am leaning on them too much. For when God is my source of joy and comfort I find I have more ability to give to the group than I have need to receive from it.

The rule must stand then: *Look not every man on his own things.* The moment I find the rule hard to carry out, I know that the dry sponge which is my heart is sucking too greedily for the love of those around me. It cannot be squeezed to give forth sweetness. It needs to be heavy with the love of God, yielding its refreshment to the slightest pressure from my fellow Christians. As I find my joys in him, so my capacity to give will exceed my need to receive.

That We All May Be One
It is not possible to exaggerate the importance of your fellowship with your fellow Christians. You need their love. You need their discipline. They need yours.

The gospel was preached to you not primarily in order that you might be delivered from the torments of hell but that you might be brought into simultaneous fellowship with God and with your brothers and sisters. Such, at least, is the teaching of 1 John 1:3-4. Such also was the burden of Christ's high priestly prayer in John 17.

The approach of death makes some men look into the future. Hours before his arrest and crucifixion, Jesus was pleading for the church of future ages. His vision encompassed you and me and situations in which we, as Christians, find ourselves.

Curiously he made only one request. He made other requests for the apostles; but when he addressed himself to the church of the future, his requests were limited to one (Jn. 17:20-23). He prayed only that we might be united, united not organizationally but in heart. "I in them and thou in me, that they may become perfectly one, so that the world may know that thou hast sent me and hast loved them even as thou hast loved me" (Jn. 17:23).

The fact that he made only one request for the church of the future indicates the importance of what he asked for. Yet as we look at the nature of his request, we wonder why unity of spirit, important as it may be, should merit such exclusive attention. Had he prayed, for example, that the church might constantly be filled with the power of the Holy Spirit, it would make more sense to us. A zealous church, a church faithful to death, a militant church, a church that could confound its foes: all these we could have understood. But a church in which the members enjoyed harmony and closeness in Christ among themselves, how important really is it?

He gives us a repeated clue to the puzzle. "That the world may believe" is the phrase he uses in verse 21. For the church was to be left on earth for that purpose: that the world might believe. Power in testimony is evidently not something that the church can possess as a sort of separate package; it cannot exist alone. The church that convinces men that there is a God in heaven is a church that manifests what only a heavenly God can do, that is, to unite human beings in heavenly love. Wherever the sign of loving unity exists, the world will be convinced. Miracles of healing, large mass rallies, powerful preaching, superb organization all may have their place. But there is nothing on earth which convinces men about heaven or that awakens their craving for it like the discovery of Christian brothers who love one another.

In no century has the power of advertising been more obvious than in our own. In three months a large company can knock a smaller one out of business by mounting a massive advertising campaign for a product inferior to the one the small company puts out. Political candidates who can be "marketed" effectively stand more chance of being elected. Christian organizations, bemused by the magic of advertising, bow down and worship the gods of Madison Avenue.

But there are limits to what you can do with advertising. You may go on selling your product, but it will be sold to a cynical, disillusioned market who buy because there's nothing else they know about. And they have to buy something. The problem is that too often the gospel is "marketed" and "bought" in this same spirit.

What are you going to do? You cannot change the whole church, but you can begin in your own life to be an answer to the high priestly prayer of Christ. You can become a small focus of change. If you are willing to be a channel of unity, you will find the power of heaven on your side. Not only will you experience pains and joys of an order you had not dreamed possible, but you will become the scent of life to non-Christians around you. The sight of loving unity among believers arrests the unbeliever. It crashes through the barriers of his intellect, stirs up his conscience and creates a tumult of longing in his heart. He was created to enjoy the very thing you are demonstrating.

I will not conclude this chapter with a Bible study. By all means look up the passages I have referred to. But let me leave you with the prayer of St. Francis of Assisi. Learn it by heart. Pray it from your heart. Become a focus of God's peace among the harassed Christians you associate with.

Lord, make me an instrument of thy peace.
Where there is hatred let me sow love;
   where there is injury, pardon;
   where there is doubt, faith;
   where there is despair, hope;
   where there is darkness, light; and
   where there is sadness, joy.

O Divine Master, grant that I may
   not so much seek to be consoled as to console;
   to be understood as to understand;
   to be loved as to love;
   for it is in giving that we receive;
   it is in pardoning that we are pardoned; and
   it is in dying that we are born to eternal life.

8

Guidance

People the world over cry out for personal guidance. Millions scan syndicated horoscope columns daily, searching for soundings to navigate the day's treacherous waters. Christians may search the Scriptures but are often bewildered, uncertain alike of chart and compass.

Their anxiety may lead them to the borders of superstition. When I was a boy, I mingled with Christians who went in for *promise boxes.* Inside the boxes were tiny rolls of paper that could be extracted with a pair of tweezers. As the box was passed round the room, you pulled out your scroll (much like the ones in Christmas crackers and Chinese fortune cookies) and unrolled it to read a Bible verse plus a religious rhyme.

"That's just for me!" someone would cry as the box was passed from hand to hand. "That's the very message I needed for today!" I was only young, but something about the whole process of fitting the words on the little scroll to my own life seemed to increase my anxiety rather than diminish it.

Though few Christians are so naive in their attempts to

find guidance, many are uneasy and uncertain, longing not only for guidance itself but for a clear understanding of how God gives direction.

It is strange that it should be so for the God of the Bible is described as one who does all he can to guide us. Such is the constant theme of the Psalms. "He shall be our guide eternally" (Ps. 48:14, NEB). "He leads the humble in what is right, and teaches the humble his way" (Ps. 25:9). "I will teach you, and guide you in the way you should go. I will keep you under my eye" (Ps. 32:8, NEB).

Before leaving his disciples Jesus was at pains to reassure them that his alter ego, the Holy Spirit, would be a faithful and invaluable guide to them. "I will not leave you bereft; I am coming back to you" (Jn. 14:18, NEB). "He will guide you into all truth" (Jn. 16:13, NEB). It is strange in view of the repeated reassurances in the Bible of God's readiness to guide that his children should be so confused and anxious about the subject.

The General Nature of Guidance

Though the Bible never uses the word *guidance*, it does talk about a Guide. You may seek guidance, but God desires to give something better: Himself. The point I am making is a profound one. It is more than a play on words.

And deep in your heart it is a guide, even more than guidance, that you want. Which would you prefer to have while driving in heavy traffic through a strange city, a complicated set of instructions from someone on the sidewalk or a kindly stranger who says, "Look, I'm on my way there right now. If you'll let me hop in, I'll show you the way"? If you are a new student on a large campus, dizzy and bewildered by the complexities of registration, it is help from the fellow student who is willing to take you round that counts, not the campus map or the written guide book.

Horoscopes fail not only because they are vague, inaccurate and sometimes evil, but because they are impersonal. There is no one to discuss matters with, no one to take your hand. For you as a Christian, guidance is meant to be an aspect of your ongoing relationship with God. He wants you to know him. Being guided by him is part of that.

Already you must have perceived that there are at least two elements in guidance that are inseparable in experience: direction and support. I may inquire for Smith Street. On the surface I am requesting a set of directions. But beneath the surface I am anxious. I am lost. My uncertainty about where I am, whether I can get where I want to in time, whether I can understand and follow directions accurately all make me crave reassurance. It will sound foolish if I say, "Are you sure I am going to be able to get there all right?" Yet if I were a child, and not a man, that is just what I might say.

"My sheep hear my voice," says Jesus, "and I know them, and they follow me" (Jn. 10:27). It is not only direction but also the reassurance of his presence that is promised. "My presence will go with you, and I will give you rest" God told Moses (Ex. 33:14).

"How very infantalizing," some of my psychiatric colleagues would respond. "The Christian seems to be reduced to perpetual dependency. He never becomes mature enough to take responsibility for his personal decisions. Not only does he have to be told what to do but he needs someone who will hold his hand while he does it."

Dependency: Yes. Infantalization: No. Like all human beings you are basically dependent, you were created to be so. Man was never meant to have the kind of maturity which makes him independent of God. Through all eternity you will bow the knee to him and rejoice over the sweet comfort of his presence.

But you will mature. Although maturity and the capacity to be independent are related, they are not synonymous. As you mature both the kind of relationship you have with God and the type of guidance you will require of him will change. You will grow more loving and trusting. You will more often *know*, without needing to ask, what he would have you do because you will know him and the manner of his thoughts.

In order to understand how this can be so, you must grasp two things about the nature of divine guidance: First, God has an overall goal for your life; second, God's goal is a moral goal. His plan for you has less to do with geography than with ethics. His supreme object is to make you like his Son (Rom. 8:29). Whether the process of making what he wants of you involves travel, money, joy, pain or whatever is secondary. His goal is to make you holy, and the kind of guidance he will give you will reflect this.

It is precisely at this point that you may have problems. Usually when we want guidance, we have in the back of our minds some overall objective toward which we are striving. I may ask you to direct me to Smith Street, but my real object is to find a certain doctor who can cure me of cancer. Similarly I may want to know whether I should apply for job A or job B, but in the back of my mind I am really struggling with vague goals which have to do with happiness, "success" or even money.

Thus when we ask God for guidance, we may have one goal in mind while he has another. We may not therefore be interested in the kind of guidance he has to offer.

It is not that the two *kinds* of goal (geographical and moral) are unrelated. Geography and ethics go together. Generally when I want to decide between Chicago and New York, there will be some moral aspect to my decision. Perhaps I *promised* to go to New York, but it will be more financially rewarding to go to Chicago. And if I may put it this simply, God is less worried about whether I make a mistake about the geography than about the morality. It matters less that I wind up in the wrong city than that I make a wrong moral choice.

Scripture and Guidance

I mustn't give you the impression that it will be simple to figure out the morality of all your decisions. In the first place there may not seem to be too much morality involved. Even when there is, it may be confusing to decide where right lies or what your deepest motives are. If it were simple to understand the right and wrong of our everyday living, you would not need the weighty volume of Holy Writ nor the promptings and illumination of the Holy Spirit to understand them.

Here indeed lies your most pressing need for guidance: The need to distinguish right from wrong in everyday living. "How can a young man keep his way pure?" inquires the psalmist. "By guarding it according to thy word.... I have laid up thy word in my heart, that I might not sin against thee" (Ps. 119:9, 11).

I have already tried to make it plain, both at the beginning of this chapter and in the chapter on Bible study, that the Bible must not be used as a horoscope. I cannot deny that many Christians, while they are reading the Bible, have been peculiarly gripped by a particular sentence or verse which has served as the voice of God speaking directly to them. But I do contend that such experiences are not the norm. God does not desire to guide us magically.

He wants us to know his mind. He wants us to grasp his very heart. We need minds so soaked with the content of Scripture, so imbued with biblical outlooks and principles, so sensitive to the Holy Spirit's prompting that we will know instinctively the upright step to take in any circumstance, small or great.

Therefore the most important use of Scripture in relation to guidance is that through the study of it you may become acquainted with the ways and thoughts of God. Guidance is not meant to come through the point of a pin. (Close your eyes, open your Bible at random, and stick a pin into the page. The verse you have picked is your clue for guidance.) It is not a celestial ouija board.

But you will say, "Doesn't the Bible speak of visions, dreams, prophecies, voices and all sorts of special interventions?" Indeed, it does. "Do these things still happen?" Undoubtedly. And I have personally experienced some of them.

But pause to think for a moment. Many of the dramatic, "special" types of guidance were given to men (sometimes ungodly and very often headstrong) who were too set on their own ways. This can be said of Pharaoh, of Moses, of Balaam, of Peter on the roof top, of Nebuchadnezzar, of Paul on the road to Damascus and later on of a non-Macedonian course, and of many others. In other instances the guidance was of so exceptional a nature that nothing less than a vision would serve (as for Mary the mother of our Lord), or the people had so little knowledge of God that they could be reached in no other way. God has something better in mind so far as your everyday walk is concerned.

His aim is that you become his companion, that you walk together with him. He already knows all about you. Now he wants you to understand something of him. The more you understand of him, the more real the companionship will be, and the more likely you are to keep in step with him, in the direction he is taking you.

The Persuasive Power of Desire

It is one thing to know how God thinks. It is quite another to want what he wants. And our wants have an uncanny way of influencing our thoughts and our opinions.

I remember an unmarried woman missionary who fell in love with a divorced colleague. The man concerned had previously maintained that though he saw no scriptural objection to remarriage, he would never contemplate it. She, on the other hand, saw remarriage following divorce as wrong... until the two of them fell in love. Then her ingenuity in finding scriptural support for their marriage excited my admiration.

The point at issue is not the morality of remarriage after divorce so much as the strange power that strong attraction has over previously held opinions and intentions. Had I been a psychiatrist at the time I would have said (knowing the personalities of the couple in question) that my friends were *rationalizing* their marriage, that, unable to face guilt feelings which would have overwhelmed them, they were obliged to cross a chasm of doubt by a bridge of words.

Since we are all made of the same clay, we share this same tendency. Not only are we at odds with God, but we allow our desires to color our thinking. It would be simple if only we *consistently* desired the opposite of what God wanted. In that case guidance would consist of doing all the things we hated and of avoiding everything we liked. God's will would be easy enough to follow, but hardly pleasant.

Yet the fact is that many of our desires are seeds of God's own planting. We are tossed about in swirling eddies of godly and ungodly wishes until we are confused and dizzy and lose our bearings.

Often in my practice as a psychiatrist I meet conscientious Christians who feel that if they want something really badly, it goes without saying that it is not God's will. Their God is tall and ascetic. His favorite word is "No" and his favorite pastime, doing without. He is the God of thunder and ice.

Who shall liberate our minds from the bondage of our wishes? If my mind is at the mercy of my passions, how can I ever use it to distinguish between a godly and an ungodly wish? Who will enthrone reason in the brain where desire already is king? Or, as someone put the question to me recently, "How can I know when I pray for guidance that I am not just talking myself into doing what I want anyway?"

Before I attempt to resolve our dilemma, let me throw in one last difficulty. Half the time when we need guidance, we don't know what our true desires are. Indeed, for one reason or another, we may be hiding from them. Sigmund Freud is reported to have told friends that when he had a difficult decision to make it was his practice to flip a coin. To their astonished inquiries he replied, "If when the coin comes down and I am pleased, then I know what it was I *really* wanted. If on the other hand I am disappointed, I am clearer as to what I *don't want* to do."

It may be then that before I ask the question, "What does God want?" I should ask the prior question, "What do *I* want?" Until I have scrutinized the faces of my desires or examined their full statures from a vantage point, how can I measure the sway they hold over the theater of my mind? Let them be called into full view. "Search me, O God, and know my heart: try me and know my thoughts."

Perhaps when they are hauled from their hiding places, God will smile at them and say, "I wondered when you were going to bring me that one." Or I may discover flaws and defects on observing a desire in fuller light, defects which are out of keeping with the deepest longing of my life. In that case, because I have seen it for what it is, I may find myself able to throw the desire away, becoming light and free in the process.

All would be hopeless if we had to do with a God who didn't care. If our confidence were in reason, we would forever be at the mercy of a sea of uncertainty. But happily God is more anxious to guide us than we are to be guided. He is perpetually active, gently penetrating our defenses and setting us free from the slavery of our hidden wishes. The problem of guidance resolves itself into collaborating with our Guide and Liberator. But we will deal with practical aspects later on.

Guidance and Gifts

When I talk about holiness, I must be careful not to make you see it in negative terms. Later I devote a chapter to the subject. But for the present you must note that God's goal for you is not that you merely *avoid* certain things. Holiness is a positive quality which cannot be divorced from your everyday living. An activity may be holy or unholy according to the motive and spirit in which it is carried out. Holiness allows for the fullest expression of your bodily appetites and your natural and spiritual gifts.

Our tendency is to label certain activities holy and others secular. To go to a prayer meeting is spiritual. To play the piano is . . . well, it's O.K. But it's qualitatively different, and it's certainly less important. Or so we judge.

But to go to a prayer meeting can be highly *un*spiritual if I go in bitterness and unbelief. And to play the piano can be good or bad according to the spirit in which I play. The question is important since it bears upon what kind of occupation you will wind up in. Is God's goal of making you Christlike consistent with a career as a concert pianist? Can you be a Christlike trapeze artist? Or a member of the armed forces? Or a business executive? Is every "secular" occupation either second best or frankly suspect, and would all Christians be better off being in "Christian work"?

It will not be long before you discover that certain "full-time" Christian workers, while hesitating modestly to come right out and say so, emit verbal and non-verbal signals which tell us they believe that only "full-time Christian service" is in the center of God's will. Only the "professionals" (those who gain their living by the gospel) are really *in*, the rest of us being second-class citizens. Sometimes we even see ourselves as such.

Not all "professionals" would go this far. Yet in favor of the view is the clear fact that many Christian professionals have truly faced the question of treasure on earth versus treasure in heaven and have chosen a pathway of sacrifice and faith, something which cannot be said nearly so frequently of the rest of us. But the dichotomy is artificial. If any distinction should be made among Christians, it should be on the basis of the degree of commitment and faith to Christ, not on "full-time" versus "part-time" status.

All of us are meant to be full time in the sense that all we do is to be done to the glory of God. And if God has imparted natural abilities to us, we should think very seriously before deciding not to develop and use them. The question really is: Can I, in view of the urgent time we live in, best serve God by earning my living and employing my natural gifts (and bearing witness among my colleagues) or by devoting all my time to Christian work and sacrificing the use of some of my other abilities?

Sometimes there are clear-cut answers to the question. The ability to undress teasingly does not call for a career as a Christian striptease artist.

Up to now I have been talking about natural abilities, things God gave me by inheritance, background or training, but which are not supernatural in nature. Before drawing the threads together we should look briefly at what Scripture teaches about supernatural or "spiritual gifts." These are special abilities, imparted supernaturally by the Holy Spirit to Christians to enable the church to function adequately. Just as your body requires the functions of your liver, your heart, your kidneys, your muscles and even your toe nails, so also members of the church have complementary roles and abilities enabling the church (both local and universal) to function as a working organism. And since the role of the church is essentially supernatural, it follows that the most important gifts in her functioning will be spiritual rather than natural ones.

Later on we shall discuss spiritual gifts more fully. They include abilities such as gifts of healing, of tongues, of unusual faith, of Christian leadership, of teaching, of rebuking and exhorting as well as others. Not all Christians are in agreement as to whether all the gifts still are meant to operate today. Be this as it may, God desires you to have spiritual gifts, and he makes it clear that some are more important than others.

To what extent am I to be guided about my occupation in life by the gifts (either natural or spiritual) that God has given me? Obviously, God-given gifts whether natural or spiritual are not to be despised. They were entrusted to me to develop and use. For some Christians no conflict arises. In their lives they give fullest expression to both natural and supernatural abilities. But since God is generous in imparting gifts, some Christians are forced to make a selection as to which they will concentrate on.

As a young physician, Dr. D. Martyn Lloyd-Jones was a cardiologist of exceptional caliber serving as assistant to Lord Horder, physician to the British Royal Family. Yet God had also given him supernatural gifts as an expositor of Scripture and as a prophetic voice in the church. It was impossible for him to find time for the fullest expression of both his medical and his Christian gifts. He chose the latter. In doing so he sacrificed what would obviously have been a distinguished career and preached in a small Presbyterian church in Wales. Later, from the pulpit of Westminster Chapel in London, he influenced the whole evangelical movement in Britain, and through his many books and lectures he has become respected and loved throughout the world.

Therefore bring not only your desires, but also your gifts and abilities before the Lord as you contemplate how you will serve him in the future. Remember that a God-given gift is never to be despised, though it may have to be neglected where circumstances call for the exercise of more important gifts. And as a general rule I might suggest that where the full exercise of a natural ability comes into conflict with the full exercise of a spiritual gift, the former should be sacrificed to the latter.

It is not that a natural gift is less important than a spiritual gift. Rather it is that we live in abnormal times, in times of spiritual conflict. Just as in time of war when many artistic and cultural activities became luxuries that had to be enjoyed less frequently because of the pressure of the need to survive, so it may be that some of us will need to shape our priorities by the time we live in. But notice the moderation of my language: *to be enjoyed less frequently.* No one suggested in wartime that orchestras should all disband. God still gives us richly all things to enjoy. And if you are an artist to whom God has not given time-consuming spiritual gifts, then let painting be your vocation. Paint freely, gladly and for the glory of God.

Counsel, Circumstances and Fleeces

You will notice that so far I have given you no simple formula for being guided. Neither our wishes nor our gifts are conclusive, infallible criteria. Nor are any of the three things that head this section: counsel, circumstances or fleeces.

Let me dispose of the least important first. If you have never heard of fleeces, skip the next few pages.

During the early years of Israel's settlement in Canaan, social administration was loosely organized. There was no central government, and the knowledge of Jehovah contained in the book of Moses seemed not to be available to the people. Pressure from hostile tribes surrounding Canaan at times drove the Israelites to unite under a leader or *judge*. At one point a young man, Gideon, was called on by God to act as such a deliverer and judge (Judg. 6:11-40).

Gideon had a vision calling him to deliver Israel. You might suppose that a vision would have clinched the matter. But guidance by vision has the same difficulties as any other form of guidance. Gideon evidently felt uncertain. Was the vision really of God? After all he, Gideon, was a very improbable leader. As the days passed and the vividness of the vision faded, so evidently did Gideon's assurance. The vision had sustained him in standing against idolatry in his own home, but when it came to leading an army against foreign invaders, he needed something more substantial.

After praying about the matter, he put out a "fleece of wool" overnight on the open threshing floor of his father's farm, praying that God would fill the fleece with dew and leave the ground dry as a sign of confirmation of God's will. God did exactly as Gideon requested.

But Gideon was still not satisfied and apologetically asked God to repeat the sign in reverse—ground wet with dew, fleece dry. Again God complied with Gideon's request.

Gideon's fleece has become the basis of a practice among some Christians which is called "putting out a fleece." In essence, when you put out a fleece you say to God, "If you really want me to carry out plan A, then please make the telephone ring at 9:10 P.M., then I will know that plan A *is* what you want." (You can make the "fleece" anything you wish, just so long as it can serve as a "sign" to you.)

Forget about fleeces. If you've never used them, don't start. If you have, then quit. Let me explain my objections.

God was patient and merciful with Gideon. And in a way Gideon's fleece-setting involved a kooky kind of faith for he demanded something against the law of creation as a sign. Most modern fleece-setters are less venturesome. They don't demand snow in August or that the sun stand still but choose something within the bounds of possibility.

But in any case Gideon had far fewer resources when it came to knowing God's will than we have. He had probably never seen a copy of the books of Moses or the book of Joshua. He may not even have been aware of how God led his people out of Egypt. His home was a center of idolatry. We, on the other hand, have the whole range of Scripture open to us and the constant illumination of the Holy Spirit. Nowhere in the Bible is there another example of anything resembling fleece-setting. It seems to me inappropriate for Christians to behave like semi-pagan Gideon.

Look at it another way. In a rudimentary form Gideon was employing the scientific method. Behind his fleece suggestion was the reasoning, "If it was God who spoke to me, and *if* he does want me to lead Israel, then he can perform another miraculous sign to make me sure."

The problem was that the sign didn't make Gideon sure. Already as Gideon lifted the fleece, heavy with water, from the dry ground, doubts would begin to occur. Perhaps it was a coincidence. Perhaps woolen fleeces *did* sometimes get wet when no dew fell. Perhaps someone wet the fleece. (Remember Gideon was going to have to lead an army into battle. An awful lot hung on the wet fleece.)

But whatever the psychological reasons Gideon had for asking a repeat sign, his dilemma was the same as that of the scientist. The experiment has worked, but maybe we can explain the facts with another hypothesis.

I feel not only that it is inappropriate for Christians to behave like a semi-pagan but that it is also inappropriate for them to design crude scientific experiments in which God is part of the experiment. I'm sure Christians don't realize what they are doing, but this is indeed what it boils down to. Please God, jump into my box and perform.

Many other less weighty difficulties could be raised. Does a phone call at 9:11 P.M. count? How about one at 9:30 or even 9:20? I am not using the *reductio ad absurdum* argument but simply pointing out that if the word of God is not enough for you, fleeces will also leave you in doubt. You are looking in the wrong direction for guidance, and you will be left floundering.

In seeking *counsel* from someone older and wiser, you are on more solid ground. When you look for counsel, however, there are certain ground rules. First of all, don't choose someone because you know they will tell you what you want to hear. Choose someone who seems wise enough and mature enough to be able to point out some aspect of your problem that you may not have taken into account. Secondly, don't go with the idea of letting your mentor make the decision for you. You want a *firsthand*, not a second-hand relationship with God. The decision must be yours. Don't even allow yourself to worry about the approval of the person you talk to. You are going to have to answer to God, not to your counselor.

The value of counsel lies in the additional data available to you as well as the different perspective of them. It would be so comforting if the counselor could tell you what to do, but you may have to go against his advice. This does not mean that you will have wasted your time for it is never a waste of time to think through all aspects of a problem carefully. Nevertheless the responsibility before God rests with you. If someone else could make your decision for you, you could blame them if things went wrong. You would have an "out." Don't look for one. Seek counsel by all means, but let the responsibility of deciding on the will of God be yours.

Circumstances may or may not be a guide as to what you should do. If you have an umbrella and it starts to rain, you will not need special guidance to put up your umbrella. If the house is cold, you turn up the thermostat (unless the President has urged fuel economy, an additional circumstance you would have to take into account).

But circumstances alone can never guide the Christian.

A door may be locked and marked "Keep Out," but these circumstances are not enough. If someone were lying injured on the other side of the door, you would be justified in breaking it down to help the person inside.

Thus when we speak of circumstances, we must realize we are talking only about *those circumstances we perceive.* There may be other circumstances unknown to us which would alter the whole picture. When Jesus made his last journey to Jerusalem, his disciples protested that the circumstances pointed against his going. He would face extreme danger. But Jesus took into account other circumstances that the disciples could not even contemplate. He went knowing that he would be crucified and that his death would provide a ransom for sinners.

What it boils down to is that it would be far easier for us to know what to do if we knew all the circumstances. But since we never do, we shall in practice make some sound decisions *in spite of* known circumstances and others *because of* them.

You might conclude, then, that circumstances will be of no help to you in deciding the will of God, but you are wrong. It is always good to look at them squarely if for no other reason than to count the cost of your decision. But circumstances can never be the sole criterion. As some researchers would put it, circumstances should be "weighted" less than morality. If for example I contemplate buying a bicycle, several circumstances might favor it (the doctor has advised me to take more exercise; several of my friends have bikes and encourage me to join them on a trip; I can afford to buy the bike). However if the purchase means I cannot repay a loan to my friend Henry who badly needs the money I owe him, then, other circumstances notwithstanding, I pay Henry back and go without the bike. The moral obligation to Henry outweighs the other circumstances.

The Voice of the Shepherd

Sooner or later you will meet Christians who say, "The Lord spoke to me about my trip and reassured me that I ought to go." Or, "My friends criticize me for what I am doing, but I have real peace about it." Or again, "I felt led to do such and such." Sometimes you will be favorably impressed, and at other times you may wonder whether the person speaking is making God an excuse for doing exactly what he or she wanted. At any rate you will have stumbled across the thorny problem of *subjectivism*. The leading of the Spirit, inner peace, a sense of reassurance all have to do with subjective feelings. How do I interpret my feelings? If I feel a strong urge to telephone a friend, how can I know whether the urge comes from God or from my muddled psyche?

Some Christians warn us against paying heed to our feelings. They prefer to go by objective criteria, the plain teaching of God's Word, circumstances and others. They have been driven to this position because of their disillusionment with the way other Christians abuse subjective elements in guidance.

I remember once being confronted by a group of earnest Christians who described to me a course of action they "felt led" to take. I felt that the action was unscriptural and morally wrong. "But you don't seem to realize, John," came the answer, "that we spent a whole weekend fasting and praying about it. We *know* God is leading us." The implication was plain enough: two days of fasting and prayer guaranteed that they were right. If my interpretation of Scripture made their actions seem wrong, who was I to differ with God's leading?

Unfortunately it is not so simple as my friends thought. It is just as possible to "psych" myself into believing something I want to during two days of fasting and prayer as it is to do so in an hour. The heart is deceitful above all things and desperately wicked. Once again we are facing the problem of dominance of our conscious and unconscious wishes.

Yet Christian experience must not be reduced to following a set of written instructions. Written instructions are very important. If you have an inner urge to do something that contradicts Scripture, you may be sure that the urge is not from God.

We have already seen, however, that Scripture emphasizes the presence of a Guide rather than techniques for being guided. "My presence will go with you, and I will give you rest." We are meant to enjoy the subjective experiences of comfort, reassurance and fellowship with God. The fact that some Christians allow themselves to be deceived, confusing the voice of their own desires with the voice of the Shepherd, must not make us retreat from the assertion that God has promised guidance as well as the experience of fellowship with him while he is guiding us. We are not meant to grope in mists and darkness for the way. Nor are we meant to tread it alone.

Yet if other Christians can be fooled, what is to prevent me from being fooled?

When Jesus said, "My sheep hear my voice," we correctly interpret him to say, "My sheep can distinguish my voice." But that is not all he was saying. The word used implies "My sheep *pay heed to* my voice." The sheep is not concerned about losing the way. The shepherd knows the right way and will make sure the sheep is taken care of. What does concern the sheep is that he obey the shepherd's commands. *If I but concern myself with hearing the voice of the Shepherd, paying heed to Christ, obeying him, doing his will, I shall find that the problem of distinguishing his voice will begin to take care of itself.* So will the problem of losing my way in life.

And is not this the fear that paralyzes us, the fear of missing our way so that we cannot take a step lest we be deceived? "I dare not move," you cry. "My heart is so deceitful. It is so possible for me to fool myself. It is better for me to take no step at all than to take a wrong step."

At this point you may make your most serious blunder. You can't follow Christ if you stand still. It is often better to make a mistake than not to move at all.

At the back of your mind you may feel that following Christ is like walking a tightrope. One false move and you're done for. Yet if the sheep strays a little, the Eastern shepherd, who knows his sheep by name, will not abandon him to his false course. He will call him, and if the sheep fails to respond to the call, he will go and fetch him. Guidance is not walking a tightrope.

I don't encourage you to stray or to take a wrong path in life nor yet to presume on the goodness of the Shepherd. But I do encourage you not to feel condemned to a second-rate life if you miss the way at some point. God is not primarily concerned with whether you wind up in Brooklyn or Bangkok so much as with your relationship with himself.

Learning to be guided is in any case like learning to sail. Recently I bought a Laser, a fast but rather "tippy" little sailboat. The winds where I sail veer frequently and are gusty. I found the Laser much more of a challenge than sailing the more stable little boats I had previously sailed. In learning to handle her I would capsize as many as ten times in one afternoon. But gradually I got the "feel" of the boat more and more, until she would fairly hum as she skimmed over the waves.

Being guided is something like learning to sail. It is a process of learning. At first staying upright is more important than reaching your final destination. If you find yourself floundering under water beneath an upturned boat, it is all part of the fun, however alarming it may seem the first few times. Then little by little as you learn how to make the boat respond to different winds, you can take a more intelligent interest in your destination.

In the same way, God's object is to teach you *how to be*

guided. You will capsize from time to time—but no matter. Capsizing is part of learning.

Prerequisites for Guidance

We have looked at several factors that can be taken into account when we need direction only to find that there is no simple formula for getting it. Since you never know all the *circumstances*, you may sometimes have to ignore those you do know. Your *gifts*, usually, but not necessarily, have a bearing on your vocation. It is wise to seek *advice*, but sometimes you will have to go against it. Your *inward desires* may or may not point you in the direction God would have you go. *Subjective sensations* may represent the Spirit leading or your own self-will. Only *moral laws* (yet only where they apply) serve as unchanging guides to conduct.

How then can you be guided?

It seems to me that what you need is not a formula but an attitude, an attitude with three related components:

1. You must share God's outlook;
2. You must will God's will; and
3. You must trust God.

By *sharing God's outlook* I mean that you must adopt God's priorities. In doing so you will become more concerned about making an *upright* decision rather than a "right" decision, that you will be more concerned about righteousness than about geography and about sanctity more than salary.

Obviously you will be better equipped to discern God's will the more you know about Scripture. Yet a knowledge of Scripture in itself will not help you. What you need is an attitude that so values the truth of Scripture that your chief aim will be to put its truth into practice.

So study Scripture. Memorize it. Meditate on it. But do all this with the aim of finding how to live a life that pleases God. In this way your mind will be predisposed to understand the will of God more easily in a specific circumstance. In a sense you will already have begun to will God's will.

By *willing God's will,* I mean choosing it deliberately by an act of your own will. It is a decision to accept God's will even though it may conflict with your personal longing. This might be compared with going on a blind date. Insofar as you may not know the specific *content* of God's will, you are making a blind choice. Yet insofar as you know God himself, your choice is not blind. You know the *character* and the *competence* of the person whose will you choose.

The choice may, as I say, lie between what you want and what God wants. On the one hand the two "wants" may coincide. But on the other they may not. In the case of a conflict of interests you are electing God's way in preference to your own.

There is nothing particularly virtuous about making such a decision. Since God loves you and is all-knowing, it makes sense to prefer his plan to your own. Nevertheless the decision to will his will may hurt, in part because it means adopting his values and priorities which you do not automatically share.

The third component which contributes to an attitude conducive to guidance has to do with faith. In order to understand what I mean by *trusting God,* we shall have to look first at the reasons why doubts and misgivings arise in our heart about his guidance. It seems to me there are two basically different kinds of doubt. First, you may doubt that God's will really is better than your own. Your own is something you understand and you feel safe with. Second, you may question your own capacity to interpret guidance.

It sounds ridiculous to say that you would doubt that God's will is better. Yet though in theory we never question it, in practice we often do. It is one thing to believe that water can support your body. It is quite another (if you are a non-swimmer) to abandon yourself to the weird sensation of sink/float disorientation you experience in the water. In practice we do as the non-swimmer does. We retreat rapidly to something we have trusted in the past (putting feet on the bottom, grabbing the siderail, hanging on to someone). Mentally we freeze, blocking out of our minds any other possibility than the familiar one. Common sense flies away in the face of anxiety.

I remember climbing up a cliff from a beach when I was young. I had no experience in climbing, but the cliff lured my hands and feet with tempting holds and breathtaking possibilities. My object was to reach the highway on the mountainside above the beach. Unknowingly, however, I had selected a point where the road cut through a tunnel beneath a huge shoulder of mountain that jutted into the sea. As I climbed my fear and perplexity grew. Surely I should have climbed far enough to reach the road by now! Yet endlessly the steep mountain face rose above me.

It was only when I decided to climb down that I perceived with horror how far away the beach was and that the descent looked infinitely more difficult than the climb. I knew I would never make it down. Then I saw the road emerging from the mountain over on my left. But how to get there? I froze. I knew I could reach up with my left hand to grab a ledge of rock above me and so proceed to the left. But my muscles refused to respond. Trembling and sweating I clung to the face of the rock.

A trivial detail assumed absurd significance. From beneath the ledge above me a bunch of nettles projected. I would have to put my left hand through them to seize it. They would sting me. Foolishly I tried to work out ways of extricating myself without touching the nettles.

I don't remember how long I hung there. I knew that I was being absurd, that nettle stings were a trivial matter compared with life. Yet only with an incredible exercise of will was I able to overcome my obsession and plunge my arm through the nettles and seize the ledge. From that point it was plain sailing.

Our fears about the will of God make us freeze in the same way. We cling to the precarious footholds that we have rather than risk the unknown. It is one thing to believe in the intellectual proposition of a loving, omnipotent God. It is quite another to entrust our destinies to him. We grow anxious and fearful as we become aware of how much hangs in the balance. We close our minds to what God would say, understanding only what we have already experienced.

> Trust in the Lord with all your heart,
>> and do not rely on your own insight.
> In all your ways acknowledge him,
>> and he will make straight your paths. (Prov. 3:5-6)

Therefore when you seek guidance, search your heart for anxiety. What makes you so concerned to get the "right" guidance? If you have a personal preference for one particular way, does your preference indicate a fear of trusting God? If so, face your fear. Drag it into his presence and tell him you will trust him whatever he calls you to do.

The second kind of fear is more perplexing. How can you be sure that you are being led by God and not *mis*led by your own desires? Who can understand his own heart? You can cope with losing money, being in danger and risk to your family. You will face all of these things and more just so long as you can be sure that God is leading you. It is this—the assurance of a true relationship with God in a specific decision—that you crave. If you can be sure of this, you will make any decision, however much others might misunderstand or criticize you or whatever hardships you might be called on to face. But how can you be sure?

Only by faith. Only by faith can you know that God exists. Only by faith can you know that he is more concerned to guide you than you are to be guided, that by your mistakes he will teach you to go in the right direction as well as how to distinguish his voice. Only by faith can you have any assurance about anything. If you are trusting him for your eternal destiny already, is it such a big matter to trust him for guidance now?

You say, "I don't trust *myself*." Precisely. You are not called on to trust yourself but to trust in the Lord. You have neither the discernment nor the purity of motive to merit guidance. But guidance is *given* not earned. You will never merit it. Therefore you must trust God to give it to you. You must trust *his* generosity, *his* ability to get through to you, *his* power to pull you up short when you go wrong, *his* ability to teach you the sound of his voice.

Take courage, then, when you have a tough decision to make. Someone who cares deeply for you already knows what he wants you to do. He takes delight in having fellowship with you and wants the very circumstances you face to draw you closer to him.

For him, the thing you call guidance is not a perplexing problem but a means whereby he may draw closer to you. It would make good sense for you to adopt the same perspective.

Passages to Study
A. Read Psalm 25:1-4.

1. The word "guidance" is nowhere found in this passage. Yet in several verses the idea of being directed by God occurs. Find the verses and note the expressions used for guidance.

2. What evidence is there (if any) to support my contention that God is primarily interested in the moral aspect of guidance?

3. List the qualities found in one who will receive God's guidance. In particular, what degree of moral perfection does God demand *before* he will guide? (See verse 8.)

Note: Though the word *fear* in the Bible does mean "fear," and even "terror," in this particular context it connotes profound reverence and respect.

B. Read James 1:5-7.

1. Your study of Psalm 25 may have led you to conclude that you will have to merit guidance by achieving a certain spiritual posture before God. What expressions in this passage would dispel such a notion?

2. What prerequisite to guidance does James emphasize?

9

Holiness

Have you ever gone fishing in a polluted river and hauled out an old shoe, a tea kettle or a rusty can? I get a similar sort of catch if I cast as a bait the word *holiness* into the murky depths of my mind. To my dismay I come up with such associations as:

thinness
hollow-eyed gauntness
beards
sandals
long robes
stone cells
no sex
no jokes
hair shirts
frequent cold baths
fasting
hours of prayer
wild rocky deserts
getting up at 4 A.M.
clean fingernails
stained glass
self-humiliation

The list is a strange one. Some items suggest you can only achieve holiness by a painful and rigorous process. Yet many teachers claim that your most intense efforts will be vain since holiness is something God gives, not something you achieve. Again, my juxtaposition of items lends an air of frivolity to a subject which none of us dare take lightly. If the means by which men and women have sought holiness seem ridiculous, we should weep rather than laugh.

More important, my mental flotsam and jetsam point to something unreal in our views of holiness. Take the items robes, sandals, beard. We picture Jesus so. Hence, while consciously aware that his robes and beard have little to do with his holiness, we unconsciously lump them all together. If you doubt what I say, try to picture Jesus with a moustache, wearing blue jeans and riding a bicycle. If you are anything like most of us, you will be shocked even though you are aware intellectually that there is nothing unholy about jeans or bikes and no moral reason why Jesus would not in the twentieth century make use of either of them.

Our paradoxical reactions are a clue to artificiality in our thinking about holiness and about God's Holy One. For while in one sense holiness has to do with the "wholly other," it yet must penetrate to the most mundane of our daily activities so that the division between sacred and secular vanishes entirely from our lives.

The God Who Is Holy

Two ideas are paramount when the Bible talks about God's holiness, an attribute which more than any other seems to express the essence of what God is. One idea has to do with separateness and difference. God is wholly unlike anything we can conceive or know. He is infinitely greater and more powerful besides being qualitatively utterly dissimilar from us and from the universe he created. Though we are made in his image, and therefore reflect his being, the difference is such as to create a chasm of endless depth between what he is and what we are. "I am what I am," says God, "and there is nothing with which I can be compared."

The second idea has to do with morality. Bound up in the qualitative difference I have mentioned is ultimate ethical beauty and moral perfection. God's holiness is not merely total separation from uncleanness but a positive goodness beyond our capacity to conceive. The very heavens are unclean in his sight. Yet it is this same goodness and beauty which he wants to share with you. He wants you to be like him.

You will never understand him, yet you are called to know him. You are different from him, yet he wants to give you the quality which most distinguishes him from you. *You are redeemed to be set aside for God's special use and made a partaker of his moral perfection.*

Knowing him and sharing his holiness are closely related. "Who shall ascend the hill of the Lord. And who shall stand in his holy place? He who has clean hands and a pure heart" (Ps. 24:3-4). Only pure eyes can see him and that but dimly. Yet if you but catch a glimpse of him, he will share his beauty with you so that your face, like that of Moses, will shine with glory.

It would be nice if I could say about this chapter what I have already said about other passages: Skip it if you're not interested. But holiness is not optional for the Christian. It is not an elective. It is your major. The command rings out from across the yawning gulf, "Be ye holy for I am holy." Impossible as the command may seem, you have no choice but to obey it. "This is the will of God, your sanctification" (1 Thess. 4:3). You are left with no say in the matter. It is the will of God that you be holy, and be holy you must (Rom. 6:22; 12:1; Eph. 1:4; 1 Thess. 3:13; 4:7;

2 Tim. 1:9; 1 Pet. 1:15; 2:5; 2 Pet. 3:11).
But how?

Peace and Holiness
Now for a little theology.

When you became a Christian, God did much more than forgive your sins. *He made you righteous.* He, the judge of dead and living, pronounced you, "Not guilty!" He now looks upon you and behaves toward you as though you were perfectly righteous. He does not deceive himself about you. Rather, your hand is held by the hand of the Christ who redeemed you by his blood. "This one is mine!" Jesus cries. "I have paid for every one of his transgressions." "It is well!" the reply comes back from the throne. "For such as he I sent you to suffer. Henceforth let there be peace between him and me. Welcome, ransomed child of mine; your sins are blotted out as the sun by a thick cloud. I will remember them no more."

The process by which you were pronounced righteous and by which your peace was made with God is called justification. "Therefore, since we are *justified* by faith, we have *peace with God* through our Lord Jesus Christ" (Rom. 5:1).

But God did more than justify you. He *sanctified* you. Not content with declaring you righteous, he began to share his holiness with you. "Not with *me*," you may say. "I only wish I could be sanctified. It is one thing to know I am justified. It is quite another to claim I am sanctified." Yet the Scriptures insist on both. They are two sides of the same coin. Unless you grasp their intimate relationship, you will enjoy neither the peace of justification nor the joy and freedom of sanctification. To separate them is to mutilate both. Consider the following verses.

To the proud and compromising Corinthian church Paul writes, "He [God] is the source of your life in Christ Jesus, whom God made our wisdom, our righteousness and sanctification and redemption" (1 Cor. 1:30). Again, "For their sakes I sanctify myself," states Jesus, "that they also may be sanctified through the truth" (Jn. 17:19, KJV). "Christ loved the church and gave himself up for her, that he might sanctify her, having cleansed her by the washing of water with the word" (Eph. 5:25-26). "Christ . . . gave himself for us to redeem us from all iniquity and to purify a people of his own who are zealous for good works" (Tit. 2:14). "He himself bore our sins in his body on the tree, that we might die to sin and live to righteousness" (1 Pet. 2:24). Notice how intimately sanctification, redemption and justification are linked together. No hint here of separation. Check the verses again to make sure. The separation exists in the minds of Christians, not in the pages of Scripture. Indeed the church in Hebrews is defined as "those who are sanctified" and Christ as "he who sanctifies" (Heb. 2:11).

You may not have noticed my definition of sanctification a page or so back. God did two things when he sanctified you. By an operation of the Holy Spirit *he set you apart for his own exclusive use.* In addition he began a process within you to fit you for divine use. He began by the Holy Spirit to make you a holy person.

The most refreshing book on holiness I ever came across is *God's Way of Holiness* by Horatius Bonar. Let me make an extensive quote from the preface of Bonar's book.

"The way of peace and the way of holiness lie side by side; or rather they are one. That which bestows the peace imparts the holiness; and he who takes the one of these takes the other also. The Spirit of peace is the Spirit of holiness. The God of peace is the God of holiness.

If at any time these paths seem to go asunder, there must be something wrong; wrong in the teaching that makes them seem to part company, or wrong in the state of the man in whose life they have done so.

They start together; or at least so nearly together that no eye, save the divine, can mark a difference. Yet properly speaking the peace goes before the holiness, and is its parent. This is what divines [theologians] call priority in nature, though not in time; which means substantially this, that the difference in such almost identical beginnings is too small in point of time to be perceived by us; yet is not on that account the less distinct and real.

The two are not independent. There is fellowship between them, vital fellowship, each being the helpmeet of the other ... the peace being indispensable to the production ... of the holiness, and the holiness indispensable to the maintaining and deepening of the peace.
He who affirms that he has peace while living in sin is "a liar, and the truth is not in him." He who thinks that he has holiness, though he has no peace ought to question whether he understand aright what the Bible meant by either the one or the other.[6]
For many years I grappled with the problem of how I could live a holy life. I attended spiritual life conferences of different kinds in different countries and received conflicting counsels and various degrees of temporary help. I read every book I could lay my hands on about "victorious living." Often I would feel that I had turned a major corner in my life and would seem finally to be in possession of the secret of sanctification. But I could no more hang on to the secret than capture a sunbeam in my pocket. A few days after turning the latest corner I would repeat to myself the words that had conjured up the precious understanding, only to find that the words no longer had the same effect on me. The fizz had gone out of the pop. The "truth" had become flat, stale and unprofitable.

If the only result had been to produce in me a wistful acceptance of that which could never be, I might have remained content. But I lost my peace. I knew I was a Christian, yet I was crushed with a sense of guilt and failure. How could God be pleased with or accept someone who sinned so much as I?

During my years as a missionary a recurring dream symbolized my conflict. I would find myself surrounded by piles of medical books on the night before my final qualifying examination. Most of them I had postponed reading so that in my dream I was frantically skimming through them, attempting to absorb in one night the knowledge I should have been learning for years. Yet I knew my task was hopeless. I had opened only three or four books while scores remained untouched as the night wore inexorably on. Despair overwhelmed me. I would struggle against a suffocating sense of doom and wake up sweating, trembling and depressed.

What I failed to understand during those years was the intimate relationship between peace and holiness (or between justification and sanctification) that Bonar writes about. At times light would begin to break as I read certain passages in the New Testament, but the passages never got the necessary grip on my mind. Only in later life did I discover with wonder that *sanctification arose out of justification, that holiness arose out of peace,* and that to separate the two was to mutilate both.

The late Bishop Ryle put the matter even more strongly.
Both [peace and holiness] are to be found in the same persons. Those who are justified are always sanctified, and those who are sanctified are always justified. God has joined them together and they cannot be put asunder. Both begin at the same time. The moment a person begins to be justified, he also begins to be a sanctified person. He may not feel it, but it is a fact.[7]

Let me explain how the principle works out in my own life. Although I knew in my head that I was justified by faith, I rarely profited from the knowledge. I dragged my feet through life beneath a burden of guilt. Often I had little heart for common Christian duties (though for the most part I was faithful in maintaining them) because of a leaden sense of the impossibility of straightening out my life. How could I confess the same sin for the hundredth time? Where was my sincerity? Having gone through "sanctifying experiences" several times, having dedicated my all to Christ, having rested in him, yielded to the Holy Spirit and trusted God to work in me what I could never work in myself, my situation seemed hopeless.

I have already discussed the conflict to some extent in the section on Satan the Accuser. Light began to break over me when I realized in the depths of my spirit that I was forgiven, cleansed, accepted, justified *because of what Christ had done for me* and not because of the depth of my yieldedness. I had preached this gospel to non-Christians for twenty-five years but had never tasted its full sweetness. It was as though dawn broke. Suddenly the relief of knowing that I was forgiven and loved lifted the load off my spirit. I found that I was set free, free to be holy. To my astonishment I discovered that I wanted to live a holy life far more than I wanted to sin. Forgiveness freed me to do what I wanted most.

I cannot say my life has been sinless since then, only that now each time I am guilt-ridden, I return to the cross of our Lord Jesus. I go shamelessly. I do not struggle to experience feelings or to achieve the requisite degree of piety. I recognize that peace and forgiveness do not depend on feelings of piety but on Christ and on what he has done. To the degree that by faith I praise God for Christ and his finished work, I find myself liberated anew to be holy. It was not that previous teaching had been wrong so much as that it never got to the root of my problem.

I have not arrived at perfect sanctification. What has happened is that I have begun an ongoing learning process.

The nearest thing I can compare it to is learning to sail. Already I have mentioned our little Laser, a boat that skims over the water like a bird (and capsizes at the drop of a hat). We sail it on a lake where the wind is gusty and veers frequently. I have capsized as many as ten times in a single sail. But I am learning. It is something like learning to ride a bicycle in the middle of an earthquake, yet somehow I am beginning to harmonize with wind and water and sail. And if I am flung overboard as I capsize, I right the boat, get in again and sail on. I am covered from head to foot with bruises, but who cares? I'm becoming a sailor.

In the same way I am learning about holiness. At one time it was only in shame and humiliation that I went back to the cross for forgiveness. The humiliation included a lot of self-conceit. Now I go back gladly. It is the basic maneuver of holy living. Now, bruised and breathless, I scramble aboard my righted boat and sail on, praising my Redeemer. I am learning to sail. I am learning to be holy.

A new awareness of God's grace and compassion is affecting me. While it does not make sin seem less sinful, it has changed my whole attitude to conviction. Formerly when convicted, I would react with discouragement. Now I praise God. "Thank you for telling me, Lord" is my grateful and spontaneous reply. "How good you are to keep telling me." I have discovered that the Holy Spirit is like a sailing instructor quickly pointing to my faults so that I might learn faster and capsize less frequently. More than this, the grace of his Spirit's conviction makes continuous fellowship with him easier. He does not convict to condemn me but to draw me back to himself. This makes for a moment-to-moment fellowship with God which is indescribably precious. I might forget him for hours, but when I remember, I marvel that he still pursues me and draws me back into loving communion again.

If you have any question about the close relationship between justification and sanctification consider the following facts:

1. When you were justified, for the first time certain things appeared to you as sin. Sanctification had begun. It affected your moral perceptions.

2. Immediately following your conversion, you probably found for a while that it was easier to overcome temptation. Set free from a sense of guilt, you were freed to walk in purity.

3. Following your justification, you had a new desire for righteousness and purity, and a stronger inclination to follow them. This took place because your sanctification had begun.

What you did not anticipate after so auspicious a beginning was the intense struggle and the dismal failures that came later. You failed to grasp the nature of struggle, not realizing that neither the Holy Spirit nor your sinful tendencies would ever reach a compromise.

You were justified and you were sanctified. The question is: What went wrong with the sanctifying process? How may it be re-established?

Crisis or Growth?

All of life combines both crises and periods of growth. Birth is a crisis. Weaning is a crisis. Puberty, adolescence, marriage and the first-born child are all periods of crisis dividing long periods of less spectacular development.

Sanctification, too, has its crises. There are moments of new insight, insight about areas in my life the Spirit needs to clean up, clearer visions into how I may collaborate with God in the ongoing work of sanctification.

However, not all crises in the Christian life are God-produced. Some are preacher-produced and spurious. And about one thing we must be especially clear: There is no crisis (except that of Christian conversion) that can *pro-*

duce sanctification. You began to be sanctified when you placed your faith in Christ. At that very time God set you apart for his special use. He also began a process in you designed to fit you for that use and to impart holiness to you.

It may be that the process, because of your unfaithfulness or your misunderstanding, has ground to a halt. If so, there is no delay at God's end. The Holy Spirit is ready to get on with his part. You do not need to wait until you can go to a special convention. Turn now to Romans 12:1-2.

I appeal to you therefore, brethren, by the mercies of God, to present your bodies as a living sacrifice, holy and acceptable to God, which is your spiritual worship. Do not be conformed to this world but be transformed by the renewal of your mind, that you may prove what is the will of God, what is good and acceptable and perfect.

Why do you need to present your body? Why, because although God *made* your body and is its owner-creator and although he *redeemed* your body, he will never force you to give it to him. He has every right to it, yet he wants you to give it to him freely. Now. By an act of your will. And he wants you to go on remembering that your body belongs to him and behave accordingly.

If in the rush of life old habits of thought reassert themselves and you forget, waste no time mourning your failure but say: "Thank you for reminding me, Lord. My body is yours to do with as you please. Forgive me for failing—but I always will apart from you." And in so presenting your body you will have presented your time, your intelligence, your volition and everything you are. You have also opened your being, as we shall see later, to being filled with the Holy Spirit.

You will not be doing anything epoch-making. Your body has been his all along. All that is happening is that God, by his Spirit, will take up the process of sanctification where it left off.

"Do not be conformed to this world, but be transformed."

Transformation is not an overnight matter. It takes a lifetime; but continuous progress in holiness is assured.

Therefore, beware of any book or teaching which purports to teach "one simple secret" of "victory" or of sanctification. There is nothing secret about the process. The book may indeed have something helpful to offer. But nothing—no faith, no yielding, no "letting go and letting God"—can begin the sanctifying process within you. And no secret can complete the process overnight. If you are a Christian, the process has already begun. So far as God is concerned, you are already "set apart" for his sacred service. And the Holy Spirit is eager for the process of fitting you to continue.

God's Work or Yours?

A paragraph back I referred to the phrase, "Let go and let God." This was a catch-phrase of obscure origins from the late nineteenth century. A college student is alleged to have written on six postcards the letters L E T G O D and placed the six cards on the mantleplace of his room. As a draught blew down the letter "D," he is said to have discovered the secret of *letting God* control his life by *letting go* of it himself.

Many people have found the words helpful. Nevertheless, they raise a serious issue about holiness over which Christians disagree. Some see holiness as a work of God to which the Christian makes no contribution. My part as a Christian is simply to relinquish control. His part is to work through me. My efforts to strive after holiness will be unavailing. In me, that is in my flesh, dwells no good thing so that I have nothing of value to contribute. I therefore trust, that is, I *rest* in his goodness. I do not struggle to control my temper but allow Christ to handle my angry feelings. I say with Paul, "Not I but Christ." It is as though, like a sea captain, I have been up to this point at the helm of my life, and now Another is going to take over. Even faith is seen as a passivity of the will, a resting and a relaxing, not a seizing or appropriating.

I want to call this view the *passive* view of holiness in contrast with what might be called the *active* view by which the Christian is called on to "wrestle and fight and pray."

Teachers of the active schools stress what they call "the means of grace." Yielding may be good but must not exclude watching and prayer, meditation on the Scriptures, fellowship with other believers, a careful effort to "maintain good works," a deliberate attempt to refrain from sin and to perform active Christian duties.

You will be puzzled as you talk to exponents of both schools to find they can give convincing and sincere testimonies to the blessings they have received as a result of practicing what seem to be conflicting principles. All schools are agreed that *faith is the key issue.* All schools are agreed that human efforts alone are unavailing and that the power for holy living must come from God. All schools are agreed that the basis of sanctification is God's intervention in the incarnation, death, resurrection and ascension of his Son, Jesus Christ, and that the help is *mediated by the Holy Spirit who brings about the believer's union with Christ.* But given the general points of agreement the words and phrases used become confusing and contradictory.

It need not surprise us that there should be confusion and difficulty. In the first place the New Testament itself seems to express both points of view. "Work out your own salvation with fear and trembling," writes Paul to the Philippians, apparently espousing an *active* view of the Christian life. Yet with no pause he goes on, "for [because] God is at work in you, both to will and to work for his good pleasure" (Phil. 2:12-13). Now if you had only the words in the second part of the sentence, you might conclude that a Christian should lie passive in the hands of a God who actively worked within him. And notice. God not only makes a man *do* what God wants. God actually makes the decision inside him, that is, causes him to *will.*

Yet to Paul there seems to be no conflict between the first part of the sentence and the second. We are to work because God is working in us. The New Testament consistently presents both what I have called the passive and the active approaches to holiness without any sense of contradiction.

Before we look at the Scriptures, it may be as well for us to realize that we are dealing with one of the great mysteries in Scripture, the mystery of the interaction between your will and God's. The glorious work of delivering you from sin, making something altogether wonderful out of you, is a work in which both you and God have a part. Trouble arises when you start trying to map out where God's part stops and your part begins. A well-known devotional hymn describes the poet's experience of a sort of progress in sanctification. In the first verse he confesses to a time when it was, "All of self and none of Thee [God]." By the last verse, having passed through, "Some of self and some of Thee," and, "Less of self and more of Thee," he arrives at the stage where it is, "None of self and all of Thee."

I have no quarrel with the hymn. If by "self" the poet refers to his rebellious self-will, his futile struggle to do by his own resources what only God can do or his determination to reserve for himself an area of his life where God is not king, then the hymn is one all of us should sing. But it seems to me that God's working and my working need not be in competition but in harmony. I work because he works. I struggle as his Spirit within me struggles. I fight the enemy of my soul as God strives mightily in and through me. It is God's fight and yet it is my fight. And the more it is his, the more truly it is mine.

One of the key expressions of the passive teaching of sanctification is "yield." Now in only one place in the New Testament are we urged to yield to God. In Romans 6:13-19 the expression occurs several times over. But scholars assure me that even here the word does not mean a passive lying in God's hands so much as a presenting of ourselves to be of service to God.

Is there anything passive about Paul's instruction toward the end of Romans?

> Let love be genuine; hate what is evil, hold fast to what is good; love one another with brotherly affection; outdo one another in showing honor. Never flag in zeal, be aglow with the Spirit, serve the Lord. Rejoice in your hope, be patient in tribulation, be constant in prayer. Contribute to the needs of the saints, practice hospitality. (Rom. 12:9-13)

Of course, none of us could obey these instructions apart from the power of the Holy Spirit. But *yielding to the Spirit consists of obeying the Spirit's directions, by faith and in the Spirit's power.*

How do we acquire the attributes of a holy character? By waiting? Or by working? Notice the curious paradox at the beginning of Peter's second epistle. He begins by telling us that God has "granted to us his precious and very great promises, that through these you may escape from the corruption that is in the world because of passion, and become partakers of the divine nature" (2 Pet. 1:4). It is all of God. And God has given us his all.

So what are we to do? Do we rest in the promises and yield to the divine nature within? What Peter actually says is,

> *For this very reason make every effort* to supplement your faith with virtue, and virtue with knowledge, and knowledge with self-control, and self-control with steadfastness, and steadfastness with godliness, and godliness

with brotherly affection, and brotherly affection with love. (2 Pet. 1:5-7)

Use all the power at your disposal to put God's gifts to good use!

Let there be no misunderstanding. Without God's Spirit within, our efforts are futile. No good thing could spring from our corrupt and sinful hearts. But we have been redeemed and we have been sanctified. We have been set apart for God's use. Let us then agree with God in the matter. If yielding means bowing down to him as King, let us day by day, hour by hour yield every part of our beings in allegiance to him. Let us reserve no part of our lives to serve selfish interests and ambitions. But having done that, let us assume the whole armor of God and by miraculous strength declare war on all that is evil within and without.

Stand then in His great might,
    With all his strength endued
And take, to arm you for the fight,
    The panoply of God.[8]

The Holy Spirit

People grow confused and argumentative when they talk about the Holy Spirit's role in sanctification. They may begin the discussion with warm smiles, radiating inner joy, as they testify of what he means to them. But if a difference of opinion arises, you will notice a subtle change. The smiles remain. But they freeze. Increasingly, sugary tones express more hostile words. The gentle counselor must be perplexed and grieved as smiling lips spout gracious invective. And before long the smiles disappear altogether. Words like "heresy," "gross distortions of Scriptural truth," "it seems to me you have not the *faintest* idea of the basic *principles*, . . ." and so on.

I cannot in a few sentences condense even my own limited understanding of the doctrines of the Holy Spirit, let alone explain where other views differ. But I would like to mention two simple facts which may not meet with universal approval but which could help us to understand. The old Puritans used to distinguish between what they called the *gifts,* the *operations* and the *graces* of the Holy Spirit. In their view the gifts and the operations of the Holy Spirit had to do with God's work here on earth. By special operations through certain people and by imparting to them spiritual gifts, God brought about his sovereign will in the world. What the Puritan writers like Owen observed was that such operations and gifts were not confined to God's servants in the Old Testament nor to born again Christians in the New. A sovereign God could by his Spirit use anyone whom he chose to.

The idea comes as a shock to twentieth-century evangelicals who interpret "being used by God" as a reward for the virtuous and the devoted. Yet the Bible seems to support the Puritans. You will remember that on one or two occasions the disciples complained to Jesus that other people —non-disciples—were working miracles in Christ's name. Jesus warned his followers against opposing or objecting to the work. He assured them that the miracle-workers did not compete with him but were on his side. Nevertheless, he warns,

> Not every one who says to me, "Lord, Lord," shall enter the kingdom of heaven, but he who does the will of my Father who is in heaven. On that day many will say to me, "Lord, Lord, did we not prophesy in your name, and cast out demons in your name, and do many mighty works in your name?" And then will I declare to them, "I never knew you; depart from me, you evildoers." (Mt. 7:21-23)

It appears, then, that it is possible to prophesy, to exorcize demons, to perform miracles and to do these things by the Holy Spirit, yet still not to do the will of God from the heart. The test of the true servant of God, then, is not being able to perform wonders but obeying the words of the Master. This is what Jesus meant when he said, "You will know them by their fruits" (Mt. 7:20).

But to return to John Owen and the Puritans, the "operations" and "gifts" of the Holy Spirit were distributed to any man as God sovereignly decided, whether those men were born anew or not (1 Cor. 12:11). The "graces," in contrast, were seen only in those who were indwelt by the person of the Holy Spirit.

And we may observe that the Holy Ghost is present with many as unto powerful operations, with whom he is not present as to gracious inhabitation; or, many are made partakers of him in his spiritual gifts, who are never made partakers of him in his saving graces.[9]

If what Owen says is true and scriptural (and I believe it is), it may explain many puzzling occurrences in our own age. Certainly it makes plain what Paul teaches in 1 Corinthians 12:31—13:3, that the fruits (or fruit) of the Spirit is of even greater importance than his gifts and operations. The latter may be important and should be sought, but the former alone are the true sign of his personal indwelling in the body of the believer.

The second fact I must mention deals with the filling of the Holy Spirit, necessary alike for power in service and for holiness. New Testament scholars never tire of pointing out that the command to be filled with the Spirit is just that, a *command*, that is, something you can obey. They tell us, too, that the words, "Be . . . filled with the Holy Spirit" really mean, "go on being filled continuously with the Holy Spirit." Thus the New Testament teaching (as distinct from Christ's instructions to the waiting disciples before Pentecost) is not to wait passively for something God will do to us, but to go on obeying a command. You must collaborate with the One who wishes to fill your being and, like a fountain of water, ever to spring up within you and overflow.

Two questions remain. How can you do this, how can you obey the command to "go on being filled"? Again, what bearing had the command on holiness?

Let me try to answer the second question first. The Holy Spirit has many functions among God's people, one of which is to mold your life to conform with God's, to go on sanctifying you. To the extent that your life is directed by him, to that degree the work of sanctifying you can go forward. Which brings us back to the first question: How do you "go on being filled continuously"?

How much simpler it would be if in one celestial orgasm our lives could be flooded for all time with the glory of God! But pause a moment. Spiritual ecstasy is real. You may already have experienced it. If you haven't, I hope you will —not once but many times. But it is not a process by which you forever lose control over your destiny. *God never takes the power of decision from a believer* whether by baptism of the Holy Spirit or by any other experience. You may with all your heart say, "Take control of my life forever by the Holy Spirit. Let it be henceforth not my will but yours. I relinquish control from here on in."

His heart will warm as you say it. But he will not grant your request, at least not in the form you make it. If he did, he would make you less than human, a sort of spiritual automaton. What he wants is someone who moment-by-moment by his own choice goes on pleasing him. As I mentioned much earlier in this book, God accepts the offer we make him. The Holy Spirit will take utterly seriously the handing over of your life and body to him. But your debt is to be paid in daily, hourly installments.

Now you are in a position to understand why you must go on being filled continuously with the Holy Spirit. It means that daily, hourly you say what Christ said in Gethsemane: "Not my will, but thine be done." Was there ever anyone more filled with the Spirit than Jesus? Yet has anyone ever had to wrestle more agonizingly than he as he faced the final step in our redemption? The Spirit was leading him to the Cross. The Father had sent him to die as a sin offering. By the popular understanding of what it means to be filled with the Spirit, the agonies of Gethsemane should never have occurred. Full of the Spirit he should effortlessly have brushed aside the crushing, dark horror that filled him with repugnance. He should have walked with a bright victorious smile to the cross.

But such an understanding of the Spirit's fullness is not scriptural. It reflects modern "how to live a successful life" psychologies more than godly reality. Following Jesus, we will face our lesser Gethsemanes. As we are stabbed by pain, we will be filled afresh with the Holy Spirit if we force the words from our sickened souls, "Not my will, but thine be done." To say this from the depths of our wills will cause the nausea to subside, the light to begin to show through, and a trembling hope to be reawakened within us.

Not that life is to be a series of Gethsemanes. But it is to be a series of choices. And in each choice we will have the opportunity of confirming our submission to the Holy Spirit or reneging on our commitment. This is why we can only remain filled with the Spirit as we repeatedly stand by our initial commitment.

Our actions and decisions spring from attitudes of mind. They arise like waves on the sea of our thoughts, dreams and meditations. Here too continuous filling may take place.

As I sit at my desk my eye falls on a magazine cover, depicting an earthquake scene. I am bored with the task I was doing, and I am momentarily distracted by the magazine. My thoughts fly to other earthquakes I have experienced. I begin to have fantasies about them and of my own part in them. Five minutes pass and by now my mind, by a mysterious law of its own, has passed from earthquakes to other pleasing fantasies. I catch myself and realize I am day-dreaming. As I do so I suddenly remember I have not been aware of God for a couple of hours.

At this point I have two choices. The one that most appeals to me is to sigh, "Will I never learn? Is it worth the effort?" The other is to say (as I have mentioned several times already), "Thank you for breaking through again. I'd do this all the time if it weren't for you. I praise you that the Holy Spirit is still within me. I open my mind as far as I know how to do my task for him and in the way he wants it done." This is a step in the Spirit. To go on taking steps in the Spirit is to go on being filled with the Spirit. To go on being filled with the Spirit is to grow in holiness continually.

A Passage to Study
Read Colossians 2:15—3:17.

1. Colossians 2:15-23. The Christians at Colossae were exposed to misguided teaching which emphasized angel worship, observation of feast days and ascetic practices. Make a list, in your own words, of acts and attitudes mentioned in the passage which are powerless to promote holiness.

2. Colossians 2:15—3:17. The passage, on the whole, promotes an *active* approach to holiness. In at least six places, however, Paul mentions *things that have already taken place*, which form the basis of an active approach. List them in your own words. If you can understand what they mean, kneel and by faith give God thanks that they are true.

3. Make a list of things Paul tells you to *do*. If you are working with the King James Version, check with another translation for such words as "mortify." Consider to what extent you can put into practice the instructions he gives.

Note: "The old man"—you as you were without Christ; "the new man"—your new identity in Christ.

10

Deliverance from Drudgery

Mia gave us a teapot.

Mia is a woman who has a knack of winning the confidence of teen-age kids in trouble. She is also observant and thoughtful. Two things about the teapot struck me. First, it was beautiful—unglazed, dull red, exquisite in shape and overlaid with ceramic flowers. The other thing I noticed is that she had spotted an empty niche near our fireplace that was waiting for something like that teapot. Her choice was a hand-and-glove fit. Mia proudly told us, "It's unique. The craftsman only made one like this."

A week later the Changs came over for coffee and Dr. Chang spotted the teapot. "Why I do believe, . . ." he began as he crossed the room towards it. "Yes, it *is*. These used to be made in a village near where I was born. The earth there . . . it's different from anywhere else." There was growing excitement in his voice. "I remember exactly how they made them." He paused and his wife leaned over and spotted Chinese characters on the inner surface. "They're very rare," he said. "Even in China. . . ."

Craftsmanship, Technology and Cramming for Exams

Craftsmanship. It has little place in our technology-dominated world. I have three handsome plastic plant pots, all identical and from the same mold. I bought them because I liked them. What care I if five thousand others were manufactured? Mine are still beautiful. The curse of technology does not lie in its capacity to multiply beauty but in its ruthless suppression of creativity. It is not what it does to things that matters, but what it does to people. The workers who pulled my plant pots off the assembly line probably felt nothing at all as they did so. But the man who made the teapot must have been proud and satisfied.

I am intrigued by the relationship between work and drudgery. Mia's teapot was obviously a labor of love. Its beauty witnesses eloquently to the joy someone had in making it. It is true that technology has made factory work drudgery. A visit to an auto factory has convinced me of this. Yet drudgery existed before technology so that we cannot lay all the blame on mass production.

Sometimes when I mow the lawn I enjoy myself. The sky may be clear, the mosquitoes few, the air fresh and my mind carefree. In spite of the din of the motor I enjoy the wind on my skin and hear it rushing through the trees. When the job is done, satisfaction kindles warmly inside me as I look at the smooth sweep of green. Yet there are days when I resent the job and do it with ill grace. Why the difference?

Working with others helps. With two or three of the family working together it's a lot more fun. The labor is halved and the satisfaction doubled. We find ourselves on better terms afterwards as we put equipment away in the garden shed. I am reminded of the black women I have often watched in the Caribbean. They sing in chorus as they weave their colorful baskets, purses and hats, threading the straw and raffia with nimble fingers.

Yet it can't be just company. Company alleviates drudgery. Slaves sang together in cotton fields and sugar cane plantations. The singing helped but drudgery was drudgery.

I think the women weaving flowered baskets enjoyed what they did whether they were together or not. At least they said they did when I asked them. They seemed proud of their work. They had the satisfaction of seeing beauty grow from their fingers. Is this then the difference between work and drudgery, the feeling of satisfaction and pride in a job well done?

Does it matter how beautiful the thing you make is? I know it helps to admire your ceramic or your weaving or your lawn. But people in days gone by performed jobs we called drudgery and got the same quality of pride as my Chinese craftsman or the Caribbean basket weavers.

Take a scrubbed wooden floor for instance. Drudgery? I've known women smile happily as the whitened boards shine clean again. Not all women, I grant you, but for some it was therapy. They would look at the newly dried floor as though they loved it. They were proud of their strength and their thoroughness, and contemptuous about the sloppy jobs other women did. The same holds true for other chores like polishing silver, making feather pillows, plowing a straight furrow or even cutting down a tree. And as the modern author of *Zen and the Art of Motorcycle Maintenance* points out, there can even be satisfaction in tuning a motor bike engine.

The subject is important for the happiness and even the holiness of us all. To one Christian student study is drudgery and pre-examination cramming a nightmare. To others it is—if not fun, at least something they feel good about accomplishing. Since most of us will spend many working hours "earning our living" in some office, school, factory or kitchen, it would be wise to ask ourselves how we may solve the problem of drudgery and whether it is possible to learn the art of fulfillment in our work.

Let me begin with study. Many students come to me complaining of tiredness and laziness. "I just don't seem to be able to get down to work," they tell me. "Then when exams come I panic." It seems to make no difference whether the student gets straight A's or just gets by. The problem is the same: Uncompleted assignments, essays not handed in, revulsion against boring texts, anxiety and feverish last-minute cramming. Some students ask me for certificates to say that they are emotionally unwell.

While some subjects may appeal to us more than others, I believe any subject, even the most unappealing, would interest us if it were taught by someone who loved it and could infect us with his love. But authors of textbooks often obfuscate and dishearten us. They take the colors from the material and insist on black and various shades of gray. Or their verbal gardens are overgrown with weeds and their forests choked with such a dense undergrowth that we are obliged to hack our way forward, machete in hand, longing for the sight of the sun.

But when we have made due allowance for impossible texts and dreary lecturers, there remains much to be said about the obstacles to progress that are in ourselves. We are tyrannized by our conceited expectations and, failing to meet them, are lashed by unrealistic self-recriminations. Some of us are immature and react to academic work much as we did when as children we were sent to restore order in the chaos of our littered bedrooms. We are rebellious children who, in psychological jargon, "lack motivation" to study because we respond to our professors as we would to parents. Or else we are fearful, imagining ourselves alone in the struggle for understanding, not realizing that many students around us are playing various forms of academic one-upmanship to hide their own fears.

And forever ahead of us lie the frightening rituals we go through in examination halls. The silences. The rustling paper. The measured tread of the invigilator, the proctor. Frantic scribblings. The merciless moving of the fingers on the clock. The increasing oppression of stale cigarette smoke. An inevitable smart aleck who hands his paper in before the period is half over.

We put the horror away in the back of our minds, telling ourselves it isn't so bad as all that. Yet our brains freeze over as the time approaches, and our notes stare back at us blankly and meaninglessly.

Changes in examination policies have not alleviated the problem. Pass/Fail grading systems, peer-evaluation and other methods seem not to get to the root of the student's difficulty.

I remember the relief I felt when I quit worrying about exams. I was studying human pathology at the time. I recall the desk I was sitting at and the view of tree tops from my open, leaded windows. With half my mind I was reading and with the other half I was worrying about such questions as: Am I really absorbing this stuff? Is it likely to come up in an exam? Maybe this textbook is too detailed. Am I going too slowly? Should I get another textbook? Ought I to rely on lecture notes? Why is it so boring?

From somewhere the thought came: Why not read this chapter *as unto the Lord*?

Not worry about exams? I caught my breath. One part of me knew that I would experience relief and enjoy my work more. Another part of me rebelled. The suggestion seemed dangerous. My examiners were not interested in godly conscientiousness but in my covering the material.

The struggle was brief and I opted for godliness. I was sick of the drudgery of studying for grades and of the pervasive anxiety that inhibited real study. I had already grasped the kind of study principles that "how-to-study" books describe so that my change of orientation entailed no change of method. Indeed I became more methodical. But the pressure left me. "For you Lord," became my motivation. To my joy I found his yoke easy and his burden light so that I studied with rest in my soul. Pathology grew more interesting. I could afford to be curious about what I was reading. I took pride in writing brief outlines of chapters I read through. The drudgery melted away and a sense of satisfaction and gratitude took its place. Exams or no exams I would study for God. And I took time off to play tennis with a carefree spirit.

I don't mean that I forgot I had a certain number of months to complete a course. But my sense of responsibility had changed. I was no longer responsible *to pass the examination*. Rather I was responsible to use my study time in a way that pleased God. I covered the same ground but was carefree and enjoyed what I was doing. I certainly learned a lot more though how this affected my marks I do not know. Nor do I care. I was no longer working for grades but for Christ. Study had become for me what making the teapot had been for the old Chinese. I drew satisfaction from the activity and from the end result of a chapter grasped as well as my abilities allowed.

Of course I would slip back from time to time. Pleasing Christ in my studies was like learning a new swimming stroke. It had to be practiced. Yet my studies were never again the same.

I hear someone asking me, "What do I do when the course material turns me off completely? I've done all I can to change my attitude, but my mind just doesn't work. Is it my Christian duty to plough through stuff I have no hope of grasping?" Of course not. Consult someone—your instructor or a guidance counselor. If you are taking a course that you have no ability for, perhaps you should consider withdrawing from it as soon as possible. Christ's yoke is easy and his burden light. He wants to teach you *joy* in learning. He has given you certain natural gifts, but he has not made you an all-round genius.

Easy and Light

I must be careful not to leave you with the wrong impression. When Christ talked about giving his followers a light burden, he was not promising them an absence of work. From the beginning of this chapter we have really been discussing the difference between work and drudgery. Heavy work can be tiring but deeply satisfying. Toil and drudgery imply enslavement of some kind and have to do with revulsion. Nowhere does the Bible encourage laziness.

I have been avoiding the theological issues and have been talking more about the psychology of work. Let me make a start by quoting verses. "Whatever your hand finds to do, do it with your might," says the writer of Ecclesiastes (Eccl. 9:10). Paul writes,

Slaves, obey your earthly masters with fear and trembling, single-mindedly, as serving Christ. Do not offer merely the outward show of service, to curry favour with men, but, as slaves of Christ, do whole-heartedly the will of God. Give the cheerful service of those who serve the Lord, not men. For you know that whatever good each man may do, slave or free, will be repaid him by the Lord. (Eph. 6:5-8, NEB)

Slaves, give entire obedience to your earthly masters, not merely with an outward show of service, to curry favour with men, but with single-mindedness, out of reverence for the Lord. Whatever you are doing, put your whole heart into it, as if you were doing it for the Lord and not for men, knowing that there is a Master who will give you your heritage as a reward for your service. Christ is the Master whose slaves you must be. (Col. 3: 22-24, NEB)

You could be misled by a red herring at this point. Paul was not justifying slavery when he wrote the words I quoted. They apply to employed free men as well as to slaves: to students, factory and office workers alike. Rather he gives us the spirit, quality and motivation that should characterize all work done by Christians, anywhere and under any circumstances.

Let me in a very simple way try to explain what work and drudgery are all about. Christians are people who have been set free to enjoy working. Man was made to work. Before Adam fell, he was given both farming and a supervisory and scientific task. He was to govern the created order, to name and classify vegetable and animal life (Gen. 2:15-20). With disobedience and the fall came a change in his relationship with work. "Accursed shall be the ground on your account," God told him. "With labour you shall win your food from it all the days of your life. . . . You shall gain your bread by the sweat of your brow until you return to the ground; for from it you were taken" (Gen. 3:17-19, NEB).

From that time man has never been free from toil, unless he was powerful enough to make others toil for him. But with redemption a change came. The redeemed man or woman is freed from the *tyranny of necessity*. The Christian is to cease from care about food and shelter and to trust a Heavenly Father. Anxiety must deliberately be laid on one side. He may work as hard as ever, but the ache has gone from the drudgery. The ground may still be cursed, but the redeemed man has been freed. He, more than any man, may discover the joy of working for love of God. And the harder he works, the more his soul exults.

Notice, however, we are not back in Eden. A glance around us will quickly remove any hopes we may entertain about that. Technology has merely changed the form by which the ground exerts its curse on mankind. He who once sweat with aching back behind a heavy plow now stands beside a conveyer belt and tightens a million identical nuts with a power tool. His body has grown soft, but his mind is weary with the weight of emptiness.

I cannot tell you all you should do if you work on a conveyer belt. I do say: Tighten nuts for Christ not for the foreman. But I also say: Ask God whether there is a job more fitting for a redeemed man. He may show you one. On the other hand you may prefer to stick around Detroit tightening nuts because it pays more. In that case you will be a slave to Mammon.

The Secular and the Profane

The "Christian work" issue came up earlier on when we were discussing guidance and vocation. Some men and women are called from their studies or their jobs to serve God in another way. Peter and John were called from catching fish to catching men. Matthew was called from his position with the income tax department to become a Christian worker.

On the face of it, nothing could be more important than winning souls and fitting them for glory. It is only natural, then, that we should sometimes wonder whether we are wasting our time in our studies or jobs. Who would lick stamps if he could win souls? Who would study applied math rather than "be involved in meaningful interpersonal relationships"?

Unfortunately we oversimplify the issues. For one thing our motives get in the way. It is just as possible to run away *to* the mission field to escape difficulties at home as it is to avoid the mission field because I am too comfortable where I am. To add to our confusion we may be pressured by the faculty (to get another degree), by parents and industry (to get a good job) and by Christian workers (to be a "full-timer"). I have already discussed guidance so I will not go over old ground. Rather I would address myself to the issue of how worthwhile our present activities are.

Several paragraphs back I quote extensively from Pauline epistles where servants are urged to do the job they are doing with all they've got. The New Testament contains many similar exhortations to people in all walks of life. *Nowhere, in any part of the New Testament is there any word of general exhortation urging Christians to consider leaving their everyday tasks for "full-time" work.* To face sacrifice? Yes. To count all things but loss? Yes. But if the Divine Commission to evangelize the world was primarily a call that Christians should leave *inferior* occupations and become professional evangelists, the idea occurred to none of the New Testament writers. It would seem rather that those whose call it was so to "leave their nets" were to be as divinely gifted for their task as they were divinely called.

Please do not misinterpret my remarks. I am not belittling evangelistic endeavor or "full-time" service. My point is that it is nowhere reflected in the New Testament as being an activity of superior quality. What matters with God is that wherever you are and whatever you do, you act always and only for the glory of God. If you seek anything, you must "seek after the best gifts," not the most "spiritual" jobs. Until such gifts are imparted, the best preparation for the service of God is to serve him *in what you have to do right now.*

Witness through Success?
Let me return to the issue of doing whatever comes to your hand with all your might. It has been suggested that the Christian who so works automatically serves as a witness to his Lord. Certainly the attitude awakens people's curiosity and invites comment.

But there is a subtle distortion of this truth which pervades Western Christianity. The idea seems to be that *success* is what convinces. If only a Christian student can get straight A's, then his testimony will count. One shines for Jesus from the top of the tree. The top athlete packs a powerful punch for the Savior; the successful Christian billionaire convinces unconverted millionaires that Jesus is real and powerful.

Powerful to do what? To make us all straight A students? By such a standard most followers of Jesus are failures and will forever remain so. The widow who casts her two mites into the offering would get nowhere in today's Christian hierarchy.

Let me encourage you, then, not to think primarily of success. Should God grant it to you, rejoice and praise him. Your aim is not "success" in the way the world around you measures success but to please Christ by the way you tackle even unrewarding tasks. Work is not your steppingstone to "higher things." It is an act of worship to a Savior.

There is a story of a monastery where the monks sang God's praises fervently and joyfully, but tunelessly and discordantly. By the time their voices reached God's throne, however, the joy and the fervor had transmuted the sounds into a majestic paean of music.

The same sort of thing can happen to your work. However mean the task, perform it as an act of praise to God. It is recorded of Brother Lawrence, a seventeenth-century lay brother, "that he was well pleased when he could take up a straw from the ground for the love of God, seeking Him only, and nothing else, nor even His gifts." Because of his clumsiness and general stupidity, Brother Lawrence was obliged to work in the kitchen of the monastery, a work for which he had a natural aversion. But we read, "having accustomed himself to do everything there for the love of God, and with prayer upon all occasions for His grace to do his work well, he had found everything easy during the fifteen years he had been employed there." For Lawrence, every action was an act of worship.

It is significant that work so done becomes lighter, less burdensome. Yet it is not for that reason I recommend it. I recommend it because *God is worthy of praise* and work is a misspent opportunity when it is anything less than worship.

Fill Thou my life, O Lord my God,
In every part with praise,
That my whole being may proclaim
Thy being and Thy ways.

Not for the lip of praise alone,
Nor e'en the praising heart,
I ask, but for a life made up
Of praise in every part.

Praise in the common things of life,
Its going out and in;
Praise in each duty and each deed,
However small and mean.[10]

So you need never envy people around you who seem more talented than you. Your business is not to excel them, to covet their brains or gifts, but to give your own abilities to your Lord in worship.

Organizing Your Time

Discipline is important. Many students fritter away their time in endless coffeetable discussions. Christian committee meetings consume unnecessarily large chunks of time. Meetings and Bible studies, important as they are, can serve as an escape from less attractive duties.

Do you organize your time? Do you map out your week's program? On paper? It's a good exercise, so long as you are realistic and don't overload yourself. Write down how you would *like* to spend your time. The result may shock you if you have never tried it before. You may discover that time cannot stretch to include all you hoped to do. It will make you face where your true priorities lie.

Hopefully it will also help you to be truthful with yourself. Don't cut out time for recreation or for socializing. Allow yourself a little extra time at meals to chat with friends. A life devoted to Christ is not an unremitting nose-to-the-grindstone life. The real waste of time comes from meaningless conversations, escapist reading, TV watching, or from sitting through long committee meetings sloppily run. Have the courage to walk out of a committee meeting with, "Please excuse me, Mr. Chairman, I have to leave now." Then get up and go. If the chairman protests, smile, and say, "I'm sorry, but you'll have to manage without me." When held hypnotically by TV, deliberately break your trance, wash your face in cold water and get back to your books.

Loaves and Fishes

My sympathies go out to the student or office worker whose talents are mediocre. I don't know why God didn't make you a genius. And though you may not believe me, the brightest people suffer the same problem as you do. They are rarely satisfied with what they've got and are usually conscious of people brighter than themselves.

It matters not how much you've got but what you do with it. Use your mediocre gifts for God. Give him your life and with it your brain and your gifts such as they are. Give him your energy, your time and your strength.

Twenty centuries ago a crowd of five thousand people were hungry after a day of listening to Jesus. The disciples were nonplused when Christ suggested they feed the crowd. Close at hand was a boy with five barley loaves and two fish, and, as Philip, stating the obvious, pointed out, "What are they among so many?" Yet given to Jesus, the mediocre offering fed multitudes.

You are a poor student? An average worker? Your abilities are below par? Don't bury them. Don't hide them under a bushel. Give them to the Savior. He calls you to study for him, to work for him with all the strength you possess. He is not concerned with what this world calls success. He did not draw you to himself because you had superior potential but because he wanted to share joy with you. Give him your loaves and fishes. Give them to him freely. No miracle may take place. But his heart will be gladdened and you will begin to taste the joy of work well done and to escape the chains of drudgery.

A Passage to Study
Read Genesis 1:26-30; 2:15-20; and 3:16-19.

Paradise is popularly conceived of as a state of pleasure without labor, where one enjoys the bounty of creation freely and effortlessly.

1. Make a list of the activities man was expected to carry out before the Fall. To what extent do these reflect God's image in man?

2. What change occurs in man's work as a result of the Fall?

11

The Fight

Soldiers of Christ, arise,
    And put your armour on;
Strong in the strength which God supplies
    Through His eternal Son;

Strong in the Lord of hosts,
    And in His mighty power;
Who in the strength of Jesus trusts
    Is more than conqueror.[11]

We think of war as ugly—and so it is. Throughout history
no war has been fought without terror, barbarity, cruelty,
the agony of the dying and the hopeless sobbing of enslaved
and bereaved men, women and children. Modern warfare
with its potential for indiscriminate mass destruction has
assumed an unreal, nightmare quality. We do well to pray
and to work for peace on earth.

Yet in our modern revulsion against war we are inclined
to forget that the same wars that gave rise to atrocities and
barbarism also produced the noblest and best in man. I
would not justify war, yet what I say is a fact. Unnatural

courage, unbelievable self-sacrifice, devotion, loyalty and love, resourcefulness in the face of impossible odds, endurance beyond the limits of human strength: these, too, are part of the picture.

Such things become the themes of poetry, song and legend. And though we may regret that the songs perpetuate the myth of the glory of war, we must not forget that just as lilies bloom white in cess pools so human virtues have reached unparalleled beauty amid the horrors of war.

The New Testament condemns the spirit of war. "What causes wars, and what causes fightings among you?" asks James the brother of our Lord. "Is it not your passions that are at war in your members? You desire and do not have; so you kill. And you covet and cannot obtain; so you fight and wage war" (Jas. 4:1-2).

Yet it need not surprise us that as an image to convey the nature of Christian living, the Holy Spirit uses that of warfare. No image could be more apt. The same courage, the same watchfulness, loyalty, endurance, resourcefulness, strength, skill, knowledge of the enemy, the same undying resolve to fight to the end come what may and at whatever cost *must* characterize Christian living as they do earthly warfare.

But I am expressing it the wrong way. War is not something that illustrates aspects of Christian living. Christian living *is* war. Indeed I would go further. Earthly warfare is not the real warfare. It is but a faint, ugly reflection of the real thing. It is into the *real* war that the Christian is to plunge. Wars on earth are but tremors felt from an earthquake light-years away. The Christian's war takes place at the epicenter of the earthquake. It is infinitely more deadly, while the issues that hang on it make earth's most momentous questions no more than village gossip.

Are you then prepared to follow Christ into the deadliest and most fundamental of all wars? I have dealt in more detail with the cost of doing so in the book *The Cost of Commitment*. But it is imperative that you size the matter up. Warfare costs. The dangers and trials are real. Don't act impulsively on a wave of momentary enthusiasm but think what you are doing. Count the cost.

Yet in saying, "Count the cost," what am I saying? Am I suggesting that it is possible to live as a Christian without warfare? For this is not true. The real counting should have been done before you became a Christian. *To acknowledge Jesus as Savior and Lord is to join an army. Whether you know it or not, you have enlisted.* The only other option open to you is to become a deserter, to hide your uniform and pretend you are someone whom you are not. Now to be a deserter is not to *leave* the army (celestial regulations make no provision for the discharge of personnel) but to evade your responsibility to your commanding officer.

Am I a soldier of the cross,
A follower of the Lamb,
And shall I fear to own His cause,
Or blush to speak His name?

In the name, the precious name
Of Him who died for me,
I'll fight to win the promised crown
Whate're my cross may be.[12]

I do not retract my suggestion that you count the cost. I only say: Read on. Let me make clear to you the nature of the battle you are to be engaged in, the enemies you fight, the weapons you must use and the manner by which you may fight victoriously. For your choice lies between fighting and fleeing, between loyalty and desertion. Therefore I say: Look well at what you may anticipate and at what is expected of you.

The old Puritans used to speak of three fronts from which Christ's soldier may expect attack: the world, the flesh and the devil. To these the New Testament adds a fourth: death. We have partly looked at them already, but let me explain what is meant by all four.

The Battle with the World

The Bible speaks of the world in three ways. There is *the planet earth.* "The earth is the Lord's and the fullness thereof, the world and those who dwell therein" (Ps. 24:1). Then there is *the world of men,* the world God loves and for which Christ died. "For God so loved the world that he gave his only son . . ." (Jn. 3:16). Finally there is *the spirit of the age.* "Do not love the world," writes John, "or the things in the world. If any one loves the world, love for the Father is not in him" (1 Jn. 2:15). He is referring to the age we live in, its values, its goals, its lifestyle.

Which world, then, are we to fight? Clearly we must look hard at what I have called the spirit of the age. Yet is there any sense in which we will find ourselves in conflict with the world of men, the world for which Jesus died? In any case, how are we to define the spirit of the age? What is there about it that we fight? Do we fight to bring about a new political order? Are we to attempt to replace the present government with godly government, to bring about a Cromwell-style revolution?

In John's mind is no such thought. "For all that is in the world," he continues, "the lust of the flesh, the lust of the eyes and the pride of life, is not of the Father but is of the world" (1 Jn. 2:16). Three lusts: of the flesh, of the eyes and of pride.

Lust is desire made into a god. I eat when I am hungry. I even eat my favorite foods when I get a chance. But if I were to live to eat, to make a principal goal in my life of the pleasures of an epicurean palate, then you could accuse me of fleshly lust for food. And as C. S. Lewis points out, to lust for food does not mean merely to overeat. It can equally well manifest itself in the spirit of the dilettante who discriminates against any food that offends the susceptibilities of his finely tuned palate. In the same way any bodily appetite for sleep, for physical recreation or for sex becomes a bodily lust at the point where to satisfy them interferes in the smallest degree with serving and glorifying Christ.

Already I have dealt in a previous chapter with the spirit of worldliness (the lust of the flesh, the lust of the eye and the pride of life). The battle with "the world" and with "the devil" are at this point one and the same battle, and in the section on satanic temptation I have suggested how you should fight it.

But worldliness is more than a way of looking at things, more than making physical pleasures, beautiful material possessions and pride into gods that we worship. As a Christian you are surrounded by worldly people, people who live for advancement, for material gain or for all of these. To the extent that you renounce the spirit of the age you live in and make Christ supreme, your lifestyle will clash with theirs. Some of them will resent you. You may experience petty barbs or humiliating rejection. "In the world," said Jesus, "you have tribulation; but be of good cheer, I have overcome the world" (Jn. 16:33).

There has been much misunderstanding about the Christian's relationship with the world. Some Christians in every age have withdrawn totally from contact with non-Christian people. Monasteries and ruined abbeys remain as monuments to their beliefs. In modern evangelical circles we withdraw by minimizing our contact with unbelievers and relating only to believers. We rely for our social life upon church-related activities, and for our entertainment on pretty cathode-ray tubes. We have confused separation from sin with isolation from sinners.

But Jesus does not call us to isolation. True, we must not

be *of* the world (not share its values) but be *in* it. To withdraw from it is to "hide our light under a bushel" or to be "the salt of the earth" sealed in plastic packages. It is also to avoid the pain of conflict and rejection. To avoid social contact with non-Christian people is to retire within the walls of the church's battlements. It is to change the militant church into a besieged church—a change the devil very much wants to bring about.

Two things, then, are apparent about our battle with the world. We are to hate, detest and renounce its spirit. We are to tear from within our bosoms any treacherous tendency to worship food, sleep, sex, beautiful possessions and reputation. All those things, while legitimate in their place, must never become objects of worship. We cannot defeat them by becoming ascetics. Only by allowing Jesus to be Lord can we win the battle. Whenever conflict arises between obeying Christ and giving way to an otherwise legitimate desire, Christ must come first.

For example I have a silly fear that I won't get enough rest when I serve God. Clearly I must be sensible and allow myself proper rest and recreation. But sometimes the matter of sleep becomes so important that I get scared. In my fear I blot out every other consideration. "Unless I insist on rest *now*, I'm not going to be able to cope later." Fear threatens to overwhelm faith. Only when I adopt the attitude of a soldier, only when I quit worrying about consequences and obey orders is my fear allayed and my peace restored. Sure I get weary! But who doesn't in wartime? "Take your share of suffering," Paul writes to Timothy, "as a good soldier of Christ Jesus" (2 Tim. 2:3).

Being in the world, then, interacting daily with our fellow humans, it is inevitable that some disagreeable consequences will follow. "Many are the afflictions of the righteous," warns the psalmist (Ps. 34:19). Jewish Christians were reminded that in their early Christian experience they endured "the challenge of great suffering and held firm. Some of you were abused and tormented to make a public show, while others stood loyally by those who were so treated. For indeed you shared the sufferings of the prisoners, and you cheerfully accepted the seizure of your possessions..." (Heb. 10:32-34, NEB). Their persecution did not arise from their self-righteousness or their obnoxious conduct but simply because of their loyalty to Christ. And while we live in a more tolerant day, we must expect, as soldiers of Christ, that some form of hardship will follow prompt obedience of orders. We must also be aware that it is now late in the afternoon of the day of tolerance and that as darkness falls, the hardships and dangers will increase terrifyingly. Therefore, while like Christ we must love the world of men, it will rise against us eventually as it rose against him and tried to destroy him.

The Battle against the Flesh
When Paul uses the word *flesh*, he is often not talking about our bodily desires but about the habits, instincts and tendencies of mind as well as of body that we retain from the time before we met Christ. In the chapter on holiness I pointed out that in dealing with these old patterns of mind, there is no conflict between yielding to the Holy Spirit and taking other active steps to overcome them. Here again an unceasing warfare is to be maintained. Says Paul, "I perceive that there is in my bodily members a different law, fighting against the law that my reason approves and making me a prisoner" (Rom. 7:23 NEB). Peter himself talks about "passions of the flesh that wage war against your soul" (1 Pet. 2:11).

Other aspects of the war might scare us, but this aspect more than any other discourages and disheartens us. And since morale is vital to victory, discouragement is deadly. Read again the section in the chapter on holiness that deals with the relation between peace and holiness. Read the section in "His Infernal Majesty" on Satan the Accuser. Of course you may get wounded in battle! Of course you may get knocked off your feet! But it is the man or woman who gets up and fights again that is a true warrior. What would you think of a soldier who in the midst of battle sat down and said, "I'm no good. It's no use trying any more. Nothing seems to work"?

There is no place for giving up. The warfare is so much bigger than our personal humiliations. To feel sorry for oneself is totally inappropriate. Over such a soldier I would pour a bucket of icy water. I would drag him to his feet, kick him in the rear end and put his sword in his hand and shout, "Now fight!" In some circumstances one must be cruel to be kind.

What if you have fallen for a tempting ruse of the Enemy? What if you're not the most brilliant swordsman in the army? You hold Excaliber in your hand! Get behind the lines for a break if you're too weak to go on, and strengthen yourself with a powerful draught of the wine of Romans 8:1-4. Then get back into the fight before your muscles get stiff!

But watch. Nothing is more important in your battle with the flesh than to be alert. Once you start to grow careless and cocky—watch out! "Let any one who thinks that he stands take heed lest he fall" (1 Cor. 10:12). For if you cannot afford to give way to discouragement, you can afford even less to be too sure of yourself. Cockiness and discouragement are two sides of the same coin of conceit. Get rid of it. You're no good—be proud of *that*. You're a nobody whom God has made a prince of heaven. Rejoice in a God who recruits bums and equips them as soldiers of a King.

The Battle against the Powers of Darkness
"For we are not contending against flesh and blood [other

men and women], but against the principalities, against the powers" (Eph. 6:12). Already we have discussed the matter at length and there is no point in repeating what I have already written. But I must add one or two more pointers. In the passage in Ephesians 6, Paul concludes by urging us to pray "on every occasion in the power of the Spirit. To this end keep watch and persevere, always interceding for all God's people" (Eph. 6:18, NEB).

Hell's legions are terrified of prayer.
Satan trembles when he sees
The weakest saint upon his knees.

Hell was so fearful of Daniel's resolve to pray that we read of all-out attack in the heavenlies on his prayer. An angelic visitor told the trembling prophet,

Do not be afraid, Daniel, for from the first day that you set your heart on understanding this and on humbling yourself before your God, your words were heard, and I have come in response to your words. But the prince of the kingdom of Persia was withstanding me for twenty-one days; then behold, Michael, one of the chief princes, came to help me, for I had been left there with the kings of Persia. (Dan. 10:12-13, NASV)

Human prayers and battles in celestial places!

In a dramatic scene in Revelation 8, an angel before the throne of God took incense mingled with the prayers of believing Christians and threw them upon the altar before the throne. Smoke rose up from incense-sweetened prayers, encircling the rulers of the universe.

But from the same altar the angel took the same hot coals on which the prayers had been thrown and flung them from heaven to earth. As they fell, we read, "And there were peals of thunder, loud noises, flashes of lightning, and an earthquake" (Rev. 8:5). Such is the explosive might of prayer.

In the chapter on prayer I mentioned many things that

can help you in praying. But there is one specific item in the New Testament that relates to prayer and the battle with the powers of darkness. When you know of a brother or sister who has been alienated from Christian fellowship because of personal failure, be quick to forgive and restore such a one to fellowship. It is in this context that Paul writes, "For Satan must not be allowed to get the better of us; we know his wiles all too well" (2 Cor. 2:11, NEB). Do not let your prayers be hindered by disagreements, self-righteousness, unforgiveness.

The Spirit and the Battle
Some remarks I have made may make it sound as though our fight is a defensive one. Let me quickly change any such impression.

At the heart of the matter is the principle, "The battle is the Lord's" (1 Sam. 17:47). How many battles have been won because of the genius of a leader. Alexander, Julius Caesar, Napoleon, Nelson, Alexander, Patton—how their names stir us! The whole of Scripture makes it plain to us that the battle is not our personal battle. It is part of a war. We are led by the Unconquerable One. And good general that he is, he knows his soldiers by name and concerns himself with their safety and well being. There is to be no cannon fodder among heaven's soldiers. The issue of the battle rests entirely upon the unconquerable might of our Leader.

Indeed we fight in a war which is already won. It was won when Jesus burst from a sealed tomb. In World War 2 when the allies invaded Europe, the whole world knew that the war was really over. Months of death and bitter fighting lay ahead. There would be cold and exhaustion, peril and pain, the crumple of bombs and the sickening death-swoops of flaming aircraft. But the end had really come. No one, except perhaps for an insane Führer, was in any doubt as to that fact. The curtain was falling. The grim show was finished.

We are now in precisely the same position. The last invasion is on. "In the world," stated Jesus, "you have tribulation, but be of good cheer, I *have* overcome the world" (Jn. 16:33). "Thanks be to God," Paul shouts in exultation, "who gives us the victory through our Lord Jesus Christ" (1 Cor. 15:57). Or again, "Thanks be to God, who in Christ always leads us in triumph" (2 Cor. 2:14).

Now there are times when you will feel anything but like a member of a triumphant army. You will feel alone, small, weak. The battle therefore is also essentially a battle of *faith*. When wracked with fear and doubt, it is "the victory that overcometh the world, *even our faith*" (1 Jn. 5:4, KJV). Or as the NEB puts it, "Every child of God is victor over the godless world. The victory that defeats the world *is our faith*, for who is victor over the world but he who believes that Jesus is the Son of God?" (1 Jn. 5:4-5).

It is therefore essential, mop-up operation or no, that we fight effectively. "Fight the good fight *of faith*," Paul urges his young protegé, Timothy (1 Tim. 6:12, KJV).

"*Through faith*," says the author of the Hebrews' letter, "they overthrew kingdoms, established justice, saw God's promises fulfilled. They muzzled ravening lions, quenched the fury of fire, escaped death by the sword. Their weakness was turned into strength, they grew powerful in war, they put foreign armies to rout" (Heb. 11:33-34, NEB).

No. We cannot sit back on our haunches. The moments before victory can see the fighting wax the fiercest. So Paul is careful about the way he fights. "I am like a boxer who does not beat the air," he tells us. "I bruise my own body and make it know its master" (1 Cor. 9:26-27, NEB). In a second letter to Timothy he warns him, "Take your share of hardship, like a good soldier of Christ Jesus. A soldier on active service will not let himself be involved in civilian affairs; he

must be wholly at his commanding officer's disposal"
(2 Tim. 2:3-4, NEB).

Wholly at his commanding officer's disposal. The words take
my breath away. Am I entangled with "civilian affairs"? Do
the "cares of this life spring up and choke the word"? Or am
I *entirely at the disposal* of my Commanding Officer? The
hour of victory is no time to fritter life away on trifles.

The last battle is on. There will be no more battles when
this one is won. You will have no opportunity after this life
to march with a victorious army in the steps of the Conqueror of time and eternity.

The Last Enemy
To talk about death is the "in" thing these days. Psychia-
trists, physicians, nurses, social workers, pastoral counselors all attend lectures and read books on the psychology
of dying. The dying patient was once surrounded by false
smiles of reassurance (and whispered behind-the-bed-
screen conferences) sometimes utterly alone as his nearest
and dearest played a cheerful "let's pretend" game. Somehow he knew he had to act his false part and pretend along
with the rest. Now he is bluntly informed that he has two to
four weeks to put his affairs in order.

Some men and women let the words float over their
heads. The shock is too great. Reality melts into unreality,
and false hope, the friend of the weak, comes to their
rescue. To others the blow is shattering. They struggle to
their knees, then slowly stand again, sickened and weak and
hopeless. I remember a Christian colleague who knew he
was dying and who said to me, "Yes, I guess I've accepted it
now." But his eyes were downcast and his shoulders wearily
slumped. There was no joy. We could not reach each other
for he seemed already beyond death, sitting up in bed and
talking to me from a distance of light-years.

Yet I have the warmest and happiest memories of a

middle-aged nurse dying of leukemia. She named the precise diagnosis accurately with a smile almost of mischief on her face. "So how'd you feel?" I asked.

"You know as well as I do," she was looking me in the eye: "It'll be anything from three to six months. I feel better after the transfusions. I'll have energy to do quite a few things."

"Like what?"

"I've always wanted to learn to play the piano but never got down to it. Just enough to play one or two hymns. We've bought a piano and I'm going to start next week. I'll enjoy the kids too. I won't need to work so I can spend more time with them. And," her eyes kindled, "I think we'll be able to manage a little trip, my husband and I, before I die."

I wanted to laugh and cry at the same time.

"What about your husband?"

Her eyes clouded for a moment.

"I don't know. It's he who worries me most. Will he be scared to touch me? To make love? I don't want him to feel afraid of me. Besides . . ." she looked away. I held her hand.

"It's so good of you to come and see me. I just wanted to talk."

And talk she did. Happily, realistically, wistfully, humorously. It had been a good life she told me. Her heart flowed with gratitude to God. She was determined to extract from the last few weeks whatever God had to offer her here. For her the Last Enemy was thoroughly defeated.

I know an old lady who shares the same triumph. "Don't let them stick tubes in me and try to make me live on," she begged me once. "God's been so good to me, and I'm happier now than I've ever been. I have so many things to enjoy here. But I'm ready to leave too. In fact . . . it will be nice to be with him forever. So promise me you won't let them. . . ." I promised.

Sometimes I grow frustrated with Thomas à Kempis

(*The Imitation of Christ*). He is on the ball in so many ways, yet at other times he misses the point completely. However his chapter on death is superb. "Think daily upon thine own death," he tells us. Look your enemy in the eye. Can you?

John Donne devoted a whole book to the contemplation of death (*Devotions*). Its complex, yet beautiful sentences held me spellbound and changed my life. John Donne so grappled with and triumphed over death that when his own death came, he arranged his shroud carefully, lay down with composure, crossed his hands prayerfully across his chest and, rejoicing and peaceful, died.

This book is not the place for me to discuss the doctrine of death. You must know already that the believer's hope springs from a Christ who has so conquered death that his followers, like him, will pass physically through the portals of death, to be raised, physically, beyond them. Read the chapter on the resurrection in John Stott's *Basic Christianity* if you want to get a better grasp of the doctrine.

Rather, it is with the *fear* of death that I want to deal. You cannot fight an enemy you fear. It was to rescue us from the fear of death that God the Son became a *mortal* human being.

The children of a family share the same flesh and blood; and so he too shared ours, so that *through death he might break the power of him who had death at his command, that is the devil; and might liberate those who, through fear of death, had all their lifetime been in servitude.* (Heb. 2:14-15, NEB) He shared your dying flesh that for you he might enter death, demolish the Lord of Death and build a wide firm bridge across it on which you might tread fearlessly.

He hell, in hell, laid low;
Made sin, he sin o'erthrew;
Bowed to the grave, destroyed it so;
And death, by dying, slew.

"As in Adam all men die," writes Paul, "so in Cnrist all

will be brought to life ... Christ the firstfruits and afterwards at his coming, those who belong to Christ. Then comes the end, when he delivers up the Kingdom to God the Father ... for he is destined to reign until he has put all enemies under his feet; *and the last enemy to be abolished is death*" (1 Cor. 15:22-26, NEB).

Defeated, but not yet abolished. We shall destroy it from the other side. Mortality will then have put on immortality, and you, like me, will wonder whatever it could have been that made us tremble before our Last Enemy.

You may conquer death now. Let its fear no longer haunt you. Look at the years (who knows how many they may be?) that are left to you before death comes. What would you like to accomplish during that time, soldier? The Conqueror of death and hell has his arm around your shoulder. "It is I," he tells you, "Be not afraid. Look, I have armor for you. Let me buckle on your breastplate and show you how to use your sword. If you grip it firmly, your hand will shake less, and soon your fear will go altogether. Keep close to me. Though I am always in the thick of the fight, I'd rather have you near me than far away. Come follow me, soldier of mine. Follow me now."

As for me, John White, it is time for me to leave you. I wish I did not have to say, "Goodbye." I would reach, if I could, through the paper to touch you. My longing is a selfish one. And though it springs from deep within me, I must not give way to it. Turn from me to Jesus your Conqueror. We may meet, you and I, on the battlefield or beyond it, but for the time it is imperative that we both fix our attention on Christ rather than on each other.

In the meantime I send you into battle with a prayer on my lips, a prayer that one day, you yourself will repeat the words of an old man, chained to a Roman soldier.

For I am now ready to be offered, and the time of my departure is at hand. I have fought a good fight, I have

finished my course, I have kept the faith: Henceforth there is laid up for me a crown of righteousness, which the Lord, the righteous judge, shall give me at that day: and not to me only, but unto all them also that love his appearing. (2 Tim. 4:6-8, KJV)
May it be so.

Notes

[1]Mary A. Lathbury, "Break Thou the Bread of Life."
[2]Samuel W. Gandy, "I Hear the Accuser Roar."
[3]Ibid.
[4]Martin Luther, "A Mighty Fortress Is Our God."
[5]"How Firm a Foundation," in John Rippon's *Selection of Hymns.*
[6]Horatius Bonar, *God's Way of Holiness* (Chicago: Moody Colportage Library, n.d.), p. 3.
[7]J. C. Ryle, *Holiness* (London: Jas. Clarke & Co. Ltd., 1956), p. 30.
[8]Charles Wesley, "Soldiers of Christ, Arise."
[9]John Owen, "The Nature and Causes of Apostasy," in *The Works of John Owen*, Vol. 7 (London: Banner of Truth Trust, 1965), p. 26.
[10]Horatius Bonar, "Fill Thou My Life."
[11]Wesley, op cit.
[12]Isaac Watts, "Am I a Soldier of the Cross."
[13]Gandy, op. cit.